Sex
and the Erotic Lover

About the Author

Mabel Iam is best known as a psycho-therapist and expert in relationships. She has rapidly become the number one self-help expert in the U.S. Iam produces successful TV and radio shows and is a keen hostess. Her books on sexuality, psychology, angels and psycho-astrology are best sellers in different countries and have earned her the Latino Literary Book Award for best self-help book *Qué Hay Detrás de Tu Nombre*, granted by Latino Literary Now at the 2003 Book Expo in Los Angeles, California. Her books *Sex and the Perfect Lover* and *El Sueño del Amor (Sex and the Erotic Lover)* were nominated as best nonfiction books for the 2004 Latino Book Award by the Latino Literary Now organization, at the NYC BEA fair. Mabel has also received several awards for her career, among them the 1999 Mercosur Research Award.

Sex and the Perfect Lover is ranked first at Amazon.com in sexuality and is a customer favorite for the years 2004 and 2005. Iam's books have also been widely acclaimed by the press in magazines like *Latina* and *Penthouse*, in newspapers like the *Miami Herald*, the *New York Prensa, Journal, Críticas, Cosmopolitan TV* and in other newspapers in other languages.

Mabel Iam

Sex
and the Erotic
Lover

2005
Llewellyn
Woodbury, Minnesota

FIRST EDITION
First printing, 2005

Book design: Alexander Negrete
Cover design: Llewellyn Art Department
Cover photo: © 2004, Christopher Grey
Cover models used for illustrative purposes only
and may not endorse or represent the book's subject.
Interior illustrations: © 2004, Jonathan Hunt
Llewellyn is a registered trademark of Llewellyn Worldwide, Ltd.

Library of Congress Cataloging-in-Publication Data

Iam, Mabel.
    [Sueño del amor. English]
    Sex & the erotic lover / by Mabel Iam.-- 1st English ed.
        p. cm.
    Includes bibliographical references and index.
    ISBN 0-7387-0825-9
    1. Sex. 2. Sexual excitement. 3. Sex in dreams. I. Title: Sex and the erotic lover. II.
Title.

HQ31.I1513 2005
306.7--dc22
                                                                            2005049817

Llewellyn Publications does not participate in, endorse, or have any authority or responsibility concerning private business transactions between our authors and the public. All mail addressed to the author is forwarded but the publisher cannot, unless specifically instructed by the author, give out an address or phone number.

Any Internet references contained in this work are current at publication time, but the publisher cannot guarantee that such information will continue to be maintained in the future. Please refer to the publisher's website for links to authors and other sources of information.

Caution: All recipes included in this book are simply provided as historical reference for educational purposes only. Those recipes cannot be used for a profit. The content is not intended to diagnose, treat, prescribe nor replace the recommendations provided by legally authorized professionals licensed to work in health care.

Llewellyn
A division of Llewellyn Worldwide, Ltd.
P.O. Box 64383, Dept. 0-7387-0825-9
Woodbury, MN 55125, U.S.A.
www.llewellyn.com

Printed in the United States.

Contents

Acknowledgments

To Greg, my husband, for his eternal wisdom and unconditional love. To my nephew and nieces Ezequiel, Mañuela, and Caterina who illuminate my dreams. I dedicate this book to my parents and grandparents who continue assisting my soul from the spiritual world. To my brother Rafael. To Greg Junior, who is the son I would have loved to have. To my friends Marta Neiva and Ricardo Reis, who are my soul brothers and who inspire me as they fulfill the purpose of building a paradise on Earth.

I thank Heather Roets for all her constant support. I thank Alexander Negrete for his ideas which are always an inspiration for my work and for being always in a good mood.

To my spiritual masters who taught me how to awaken my inner self and expand my awareness, especially master Meishu Sama. To a soul gardener and teacher: Carl Jung.

To all those who dream about building a better world. To my loyal readers.

I dedicate this book to all with the infinite wish that Divine Love will form part of our lives and bring a powerful blessing to each person who reads these pages.

Magic is to live, communicate, think,
and express ourselves to
feel and discover the eternal secrets of our existence.
Sexual magic is the encounter of two universes:
the feminine and the masculine;
this union results in love, creation,
wisdom and happiness;
ecstasy, power, and life.

Mabel Jam

Introduction

The Divine Magic of Love

Is there a key to achieving ecstasy as lovers no matter how long the relationship? Can we recreate sexual attraction toward the people we desire? Can our problems as a couple be resolved through the magical art of sex?

Sexual magic creates a state of ecstasy beyond the restrictions of our mind and body. It gives us the opportunity to resolve our problems as a couple in time of crisis, thus achieving a state of total and transcendental plenitude. Sexual magic is awareness of the use of sexual energy. In the old times, sexual magic was taught in secret initiation temples. According to some followers, this art was only taught to clever disciples, indicating the importance and the seriousness required to master this subject.

This has nothing to do with becoming sexual gymnasts or mystics with a passion for sex. The objective is to enter into a world of perceptions and sensibilities to which the common person has no access. To do it, we must change the way we think and feel about sexuality. The techniques offered by sexual magic are normally unknown to most of us.

The purpose of this book is to discover the intimate relationship between sexuality and spiritual ecstasy, so as to achieve a unique and divine relationship and to develop spiritual growth through love and sex. This will bring us fulfillment in all aspects of life as partners and lovers.

Sexual pleasure is part of the spiritual path, in spite of Western culture's condemnation of sex as a simple, mechanical act concerned only with genital pleasure. For the sacred lover or magical sexual partner, love is art, poetry, music, ecstasy, trance, devotion, adoration, and surrender.

The secret lies in the sexual energy—that energy that comes from our real self, and lives in the inner space which holds the perfect spirit of the wholeness of life. Many of us have been taught that what we feel about sex is not acceptable and, consequently, we deny and mistrust our own experience.

These magical techniques lead us to simply trust the natural aspect of our feelings and be true to ourselves. They show us how to surrender to our feelings and our sexuality—instead of suppressing or controlling them—which are the basis of true pleasure and spiritual development.

Making love should be like a dance, where two partners who love each other feel that they are attuned to a harmonious melody that takes them to a total union. In that relaxation, in that deep surrender, they start a new consciousness where they can discover the secrets of a divine existence. Thus, sex becomes a gift of life.

Dare to achieve magic with eroticism. This book will guide you through the steps of personal fulfillment, as a human being and as a couple; it will allow you to grow as a spiritual being and to achieve fulfillment in all aspects of your life.

The fundamental message throughout this book is the goal aspired to by each human being: to achieve profound happiness.

To love is to travel beyond imagination through the
magic and celestial melody of the stars.
To love is to live the adventure, and to explore
deep into our hearts.

Mabel Jam

Chapter 1

The Magical Art of Love

Magic is the art of using the energies found in nature and the universe. To perform magic we need to understand the spiritual laws that govern the material world. Spiritual forces operate and drive this material world, but this is a truth that most people ignore.

By "sexual magic," we mean awareness of the conscious use of sexual energy. Sexual magic does not endorse the absurd idea of having a linear sexual relationship in which both partners search for something called orgasm. An orgasm is more than the sensation of relief generated when energy is no longer blocked. Any blocked energy when liberated produces pleasure, and therefore is gladly accepted. However, in this book we are trying to go deeper than that.

Magical ecstasy is the experience of sexuality as a spiritual communion with our partner. It allows us to fuse ourselves with our inner divinity, or oneness, and with our real and eternal self. In order to successfully experience sexual magic, there are four main factors that must occur:

The first one refers to the extrasensory communication that takes place during intercourse, through the heightening of the senses that can perceive beyond the obvious. For example, the existing non-verbal attunement between partners.

The second one relates to the high mental sensitivity we have before, during, and after intercourse, as people concentrate on the sexual act they become vulnerable to any positive or negative stimulus.

The third factor is connected to the awakening of sexuality; stimulating the unconscious levels of a person's psyche, the astral worlds or deep spiritual states. This is proven by the frequency and intensity of dreams or visions that may appear after the sexual act.

The last factor states that those who practice Tantra (a means of expansion of the ordinary consciousness to access divine consciousness, and also a series of sacred Hindu books which describe certain rituals, disciplines, and sexual meditations) also experience during intercourse what is known as *samadhi*, the perception of eternity and the total dissolution of the ego.

To reach those phases successfully and to obtain a deep spiritual contact with our magical partner, we must understand certain laws. The laws mentioned here will be expanded, explained and developed in detail throughout the book:

Create a magical, sacred space.

Prepare your home or erotic place in a harmonious and magical way using specific methods such as feng shui.

Learn magical rituals.

Know the erotic zones and their anatomic functions.

Learn to meditate and visualize to control mental energy.

Develop sexual creativity and magnetism.

Learn how to liberate and harmonize your energy centers through meditation.

Know how physical, emotional, and mental energy work.

Practice exercises to balance the centers of energy.

Use your five senses with intelligence.

Perform visualizations to manage sexual energy in a magical way.

Learn which colors and symbols help deepen sexual magic.

Practice different erotic techniques and positions to enhance pleasure.

Use and take advantage of unconscious erotic energy through the knowledge of dreams and their symbology.

Organize and balance your thoughts and emotions so as to resolve sexual barriers in your relationship with your partner.

Learn the secrets to achieve happiness and fulfillment.

Sexual magic comes from the same principle as many Eastern techniques: Human sexuality has deeper implications than mere procreation. When performing any magical act, the couple becomes aware of their mutual needs, which strengthens their spiritual bond and thus the sexual act becomes deeper and more regenerating. In this way we achieve the psychological integration necessary to separate ourselves from our cultural biases and unconscious beliefs imposed by everyday life.

The key to beginning this adventure is to be in love with our partner, whom we call our "magical partner." As in other spiritual paths, sacred or magical sex teaches us the discipline of mind and body which allows us to celebrate the sensual aspects of life.

The strongest energy of human beings is sexual energy. Most people do not know how to control that energy since it has been separated from the spiritual process, creating an obsessive mental process and, thus, resulting in behaviors lacking harmony in the sexual relationships of most couples. Sexual magic looks for a path to unify the divine within us through sexual energy.

Benefits we achieve when we practice sexual magic:

1. We experience each encounter as a unique event.

2. We achieve authenticity and total openness during erotic encounters.

3. We pay homage to the universe by celebrating each sexual act.

4. We create a positive resonance in our relationship, beyond physical attraction.

5. We experience the energy of love at the present moment, understanding the true meaning of life.

6. We make our dreams and desires as a couple come true.

7. We experience sex as something sacred.

8. We make positive, creative, and magical choices at each moment.

9. We experience total and plentiful openness.

10. We create a divine relationship with our partner.

Create a Magical Space for Love

"I dream of being alone together in a secret paradise away from this world. Both of us are surrounded by volcanic lands and sweet, crystal waters. The whisper of our entangled bodies is the music around us, in that sacred space, beyond the sun."

When a couple lives together it is essential to have a space that suits their tastes, where they both feel protected and at ease. To select the area where you will establish your sacred erotic space you must pay attention to your intuition.

Discuss it with your magic partner and take steps to create that intimate space. If possible, it should be an almost secret place, out of sight of all the other areas of the home. You must visualize it and decide what you would like to place there. Think about items that are important or meaningful to your or your partner. Your sacred space will be a place where you can experience who you are and who you would like to be, where you can transcend your everyday needs and, thus, illuminate your spirit.

A home, like the body, needs the correct use of color, light, furniture, and objects to suit your style of living. This space must have objects and spaces that permanently awaken romance and sensuality. For example, in the bedroom you may place plants with intertwined trunks, photos of you and your partner during a happy event, a sculpture portraying lovers embracing each other.

Most importantly, a sacred place must have an altar. Building a sacred place is a creative process (the word "create" comes from Latin and means "to be"). When we build an altar within our sacred space, it gives physical shape and form to our inner feelings and thoughts.

The altar can be mounted on a small wood table, and can include a metal candelabra, a small bowl with dirt or salt, a glass or a container with water, perfumes, plants, flowers, incense, a sacred symbol or image, and a candle. Some people declare that the preparation and setting up of the altar generates the energy needed to start a sexual magic ritual.

The way we decide to use our own sacred space and the role it plays in our everyday life is, by its nature, private and personal. For that reason it is not surprising that there are so many significant differences in the way people energize that space. You can perform strict rituals to purify this site, fumigating with herbs or consecrating the altar with ceremonies performed at specific times (for example, the full moon, the equinoxes or solstices). You can burn incense or oils, play a drum or ring bells.

As time passes, you will discover that your practices may change as you develop your spiritual vocabulary, starting with formal purification and cleansing rituals and ending with simple invocations or prayers. The way that sacred space is energized will depend on the style and customs of each person.

Here are some suggestions to energize and renew the sacred space daily:

Fumigate or burn incense.

Play a drum or any other musical instrument (this helps to elevate the vibrations of the place).

Ring a bell.

Sing a song.

Add some flowers.

Add a container with water.

Place crystals and gems on the altar.

Add pictures of spiritual masters.

Add sacred writings or texts.

Include cards with words or drawings that describe your wishes or
aspirations.

Place colored candles on the altar.

Include objects that invoke love or sacred memories.

Add photos of the people we love or of happy times.

The utilization of a sacred place helps us set aside our daily worries
(the pending phone call, the business transaction that did not come
through, our children's demands) and it allows us to concentrate on the
magical work that the couple desires to perform.

As you create or build the altar with your partner or alone, remember
something that has given you deep pleasure: A walk under the rain, a
majestic sight, a dance, a moment of bliss with your partner, a meditation, an erotic encounter, a surprise, a gift. If you create this space together, both of you must decide the type of activity or ambiance you
would like to achieve and which sacred objects will be introduced to that
space. Once you have created the desired environment, decide what you
would like to experience or share.

At the end of each magic work, remember to clean or renovate the altar. When we take down an altar built for a specific purpose, we find a
feeling of closure and the start of a new period in the relationship of the
magical couple.

Eroticism and Feng Shui

To attract love, or to maintain and improve your present relationship,
work on the design or decoration of a space full of warmth and trust.
These are the two basic concepts that are at the heart of excellent communication. To balance that sacred space and achieve total success, we
can use some principles of the art of feng shui. This is the most suitable
technique to preserve a magical love and an everlasting relationship.

Feng shui means "soft winds over calm waters" and originated in China. It analyzes the daily interaction we have with our environment: our
home, our city, or our workplace. The basic premise is that if we establish a harmonious, cooperative relationship with our environment, we

increase our chances of achieving success in all areas of life: health, relationships, and prosperity.

Feng shui has its roots in the Taoist philosophy. With more than twenty-five hundred years of history, it also incorporates elements of Buddhism. Today we find three different approaches within feng shui: *Traditional* feng shui, related to Chinese astrology; *Buddhist* feng shui, based on the observation of forms and the chi or the flow of vital energy; and *rational* feng shui that incorporates art principles into the design of contemporary and Eastern environments.

Feng shui, also known in China as "the art of placement" or the "cure from Heaven," is the science of the conscious organization of space, materials and living beings involved in everyday life, work, and pleasure. It harmonizes the mutual interdependency between us and the cosmos. Chinese culture recognizes five forces that form all that exists in nature: earth, water, wood, metal, and fire. These energies can give life or destroy. Each element, in its different representations, may bring its qualities to decorate a space that connects us to our unconscious needs.

Earth is associated with fertility, maternity, and abundance; with a feeling of home. It is excellent for attracting stability and safety in a romance, encouraging a tender, warmer, more fraternal sexual relationship. What can be used to create this type of ambiance? Ceramic and porcelain objects, earthen colors, neutral colors, yellows, textiles with a thick and heavy texture or with square patterns, light with yellow tones, and short, small plants such as violets and orange or yellow flowers.

Metal is the element associated with order, clarity, cleanness, rectitude and romance. It is excellent for clarifying and putting our thoughts in order, and for establishing a frank, open, direct and solid, love relationship, although it may fall into superficiality and lack of expression. We can use metal objects and sculptures to create this type of environment, with circular forms, colors such as white, soft whites and pastels, textiles with circular drawings or firm textures such as satin or taffeta, plants with rounded leaves, and flowers in shades of white and pastels.

Water is the element that relates to our deep thoughts, and our sense of adventure and freedom. In excess, water can bring solitude. It is recommended to enhance communication, freedom, adventure, and sexual activity in a deep relationship that is full of feelings but lacking in passion. To create this type of environment, we can use fountains, fish bowls or tanks, mirrors, asymmetrical and undulating forms, landscapes with lakes and rivers, soft textiles such as chiffon and gauze, dark colors such as grey, navy blue, dark purple or shades of wine, plants with uneven, undulating leaves, and flowers in shades of blue or purple.

Wood is the element associated with creativity, impulses, freshness, and growth that will nourish an innocent, immature relationship, full of constant changes, strong impulses, frankness, and vanity. In excess, it may lead to immaturity, constant arguments, and ego fights. The objects suggested to attract this type of energy are plants, elongated shapes such as columns, shades of green, textiles made of fibers such as linen or cotton with rectangular or elongated patterns, and fabrics with horizontal or vertical stripes.

Fire is the element that represents spontaneity, passion, joy, fame, and festivities, aspects it will reflect in a sexual relationship full of constant ups and downs, and in an excess of emotions in a passionate but short-lived relationship. This environment can be created with candles, lamps, textiles such as silk, wool, furs, feathers; bright red, orange, and yellow colors; red flowers and plants with triangular-shaped leaves.

Another important aspect to consider when designing an attractive sexual environment is the distribution of the furniture, ornaments and pictures or sculptures as well as the type of bed in the bedroom. Here are twenty recommendations that support the goals of sexual magic:

1. A bedroom, to promote eroticism, must be oriented toward the south. The door, the window or at least the bed headboard must look toward the south. Stand with your back against the entrance door looking inside the bedroom and use a compass to find the cardinal directions.

2. According to feng shui, the south is a pole of great energy, as in that hemisphere we receive energy from a constellation called the Southern Cross. If it is impossible to turn the headboard of the bed toward that cardinal point, place a mirror so that it will be reflected there. If you do not like mirrors, you could use an ornament with a reflective surface to absorb the pole in question. The

partner who needs to have more energy should face the mirror that reflects the south.

3. The bedroom must receive sunlight during the day. Open the curtains or shades so that the bed can be exposed to the sun. If you live in a dark area, there is a solution: Turn the lights on for at least an hour and a half during the day. There is no need to turn the light on when the partners meet. You can charge the bed during the day and turn the light off at night. Light represents energy the same as running water. This recharges the chi, or positive spirit, in the place. Do not let the negative spirit, the sha, accumulate and fill the place.

4. Elements with pointed shapes generate more energy. A pyramid, a beam, or a right angle all energize and inspire eroticism. If possible, put away the point-shaped object during sleep hours, as this will reduce the energy so you can fall asleep more easily and rest better.

5. Include some material derived from animals since animals relate to the element of fire (energy): leather, furs, wool carpets, leather masks, or fur bedspreads, for example. It is not necessary to have this element on the bed; it may be represented by small ornaments.

6. Select natural fabrics in your decorating, such as natural silk or cotton for the sheets. Silk brings out eroticism.

7. Do not use polyester. Even though this material is very practical when it comes to washing and ironing, unfortunately it does not produce any energy since it is synthetic.

8. The mirrors do not need to reflect the bodies of the partners.

9. Fire is an element that must be present in the room. We do not need a fireplace, although it would be ideal. We can obtain good results from candelabra, red candles, or burners for incense or spices.

10. On the male's night table, place a tiny jar with copper scraps. This element represents the male essence and it is fundamental to enhancing eroticism to its fullness. This copper can be bought in

Asian stores.

11. On the female's night table there should be a plant with red flowers — fresh, not artificial. Plants have to be natural and, in the case of flowers, they have to be fresh and kept in water. Red flowers and plants with red flowers increase eroticism in the female partner.

12. The slippers you wear to walk in the bedroom should not be the same you wear to walk in any other areas of the home. Why? Very simple: they get charged with energy. That is why people in the East remove their shoes before entering their homes. If you wish to have a night full of sex, try to leave behind all the energy you have accumulated during the day.

13. There must be nothing underneath the bed. It is important to leave that space open to release energy into the environment.

14. When the partners enter the bedroom they should wear a perfume that identifies each of them, but during the day you must try to burn incense or oils with intense aromas like sandalwood or patchouli.

15. Hang a mobile in the room to renew and activate the energy. The mobile must make a harmonious sound when moving. It must be pleasing to the ear and be in a place where it can be in continuous motion. Near a window or attached to a door, for example, produces good results.

16. You should never look at the bathroom from the bed. If there is a bathroom adjoining the bedroom, just close the door.

17. The walls between the bed and the bathroom conduct negative energy, but there is a remedy for that. Copper filings and plants with red flowers are ideal to form a protective "fence" against the shared wall.

18. If the bedroom is well lit, there is no need to take any special care about the colors of the walls. If the room is dark, then you must have something in shades of red.

19. If the couple feels less energy and eroticism, then it is time to ren-

ovate the bedroom. There is no need to redecorate every day, but you can change the placement of the ornaments or the cushions. That is enough.

20. To preserve sexual receptivity, the couple may place a ruby or a garnet either hanging over the night table or on it. These stones are very energizing and powerful when trying to attract the opposite sex.

Color is our best ally to make us feel at ease with the decoration of a home. Thus, it is helpful to use it according to our personalities and the needs of the couple. If both are calm and quiet, warm colors in the bedroom will increase their passion. On the contrary, if they wake up often or find it difficult to go to sleep, it is better to use soft colors and use some candles or soft lights.

As for colors, I recommend warm colors for the bedroom. A soft light by the sofa, the fire in a fireplace, the reflections of a candle, all create an ideal environment. As for tastes, consider good food and aphrodisiac elements. For the tactile, consider silk, velvet, cotton, and leather. The smells of jasmine, roses, patchouli or lavender, and the sounds of nature, such as waterfalls or sea waves, are easy to find. You can also consider jazz or classical music.

Sensuality can be developed according to what we perceive through our senses: the aroma of orange blossoms, the sound of rain on the roof. The world in general is formed by small details that give us the gift of pleasure. The aromas, tastes, and colors that invoke romanticism can create a wonderful home environment and thus transform the space for the couple to enjoy each other with plenitude.

Exercise: Feel Happiness at Home

Write a list of plants (trees, bushes, or any other type) that bring memories of your childhood, or a happy moment in your life. Try to find positive associations; for example, a plant with a certain flower may remind you of the garden where you used to play as a child. Think of a texture you would like to feel over your skin. Also think about aromas that evoke positive emotions. Which are your favorite sounds of nature: the sound of the waves or the sound of the wind blowing leaves? Are those plants, sounds, aromas, or textures present in your bedroom or in your sacred space?

With a few exceptions, we all enjoy natural landscapes. We feel their perfect balance, and when contemplating them, we nurture and invigorate ourselves and reach a very special inner balance and state. We all form part of nature. One of the essences of feng shui, thus, is to recreate our sensory experiences from nature within our home. A pleasant place is characterized by the variety of stimuli for our senses that open our heart to beauty.

Love Rituals to Fulfill Our Dreams

Once our space has achieved harmony and has been decorated to create ambiance, we can begin to perform rituals to heighten eroticism. This way, we will energize the place as well as the bond of love.

Erotic rituals can have marvelous effects on a couple, and the possibility of performing them as truly creative acts may deeply change the purpose of lovemaking. The ritual has a nurturing function and it does not need to be performed in a formal way. That is why it should be simple and attractive from an aesthetic and spiritual point of view. It must be flexible and involve all our senses. The sexual ritual is simple, but it must be performed with harmony and with a sacred attitude so as to be considered a ritual.

Breathing Rituals for a Couple

When we learn how to breathe, our body finds a state of vital balance and relaxation. Breathing correctly consists of working both the lungs as well as the abdomen to achieve a deep, complete breath. The couple must lie on a comfortable surface and be uninterrupted for fifteen to thirty minutes. At the beginning, until our respiration becomes natural and fluid, it is better to practice this exercise while the body rests.

Pay attention to your thoughts and let them be free and pass by like a rain of energy. Do not identify yourself with any type of thought. After a few minutes of relaxation, place one hand on your abdomen and the other one on your chest. Exhale softly all the air through the nose, emptying your lungs completely. Try to keep your lungs empty for a few seconds. Inhale slowly, inflating only the abdomen till it gets to the lower part of the lungs. Without any effort, you will feel the diaphragm expanding below. At this moment, the lower and middle areas of the lungs are full of air.

Before exhaling, clear your thoughts and imagine that you are clearing your emotions and daily tensions. Then move the air to the upper part of the lungs by contracting the abdomen slightly and slowly expelling the air. Repeat this process for at least ten minutes. The correct respiration will create a balance between the energies and the negative and positive polarity; it will soothe your nerves and regulate the heartbeat. Thus it reduces blood pressure and stimulates digestion.

This breathing exercise increases the flow of vital energy:

1. Inhale slowly through the nose counting to seven.
2. Exhale slowly through the nose counting to seven.
3. Inhale slowly through the nose counting to seven.
4. Hold your breath counting to seven.
5. Exhale slowly through your mouth counting to seven.

As you inhale, imagine a feeling of harmony, love, and increase of energy. As you exhale, visualize all the negative forces leaving your body and mind.

Ritual for Mental and Physical Relaxation

Many people can reach a state of deep relaxation any time. Others may find that the simple idea of relaxing causes them to be more tense. Better results may be achieved with a relaxation ritual performed while lying on the bed for at least ten minutes. Follow these instructions:

Lie comfortably on your bed with your eyes closed; control your breathing to reach a deep stage. Progressive relaxation allows us to identify which muscles in our body are tense and teaches us to distinguish between feeling tense or feeling a deep relaxation. We must identify the four main groups of muscles and follow systematically the sequence of contraction/relaxation. Each muscle or group of muscles tenses for about five to seven seconds and later relaxes for twenty to thirty seconds. The more you practice, the better and faster the relaxation. At the beginning it may seem difficult to relax one or several muscles (the head and neck muscles seemed to be more "charged"). If you feel them tense, repeat (in your mind or in a low voice) a phrase like: "I release all tension," or "I am calmed and relaxed."

Start with the hand muscles, the forearms and the biceps. Close both fists, tense your biceps and forearms, then relax.

Continue with the head muscles, the face, the neck and the shoulders. Frown and move your head in a complete circle, first clockwise and then counter-clockwise. Wrinkle your face, the space between your eyebrows, tighten your lips, push your tongue against the palate, and shrug your shoulders. Then relax.

Continue with the thorax muscles, the stomach and the lumbar area. Spread your shoulders and arch your back as if breathing. Keep that posture. Relax. Inhale deeply, tightening the stomach area. Hold this posture. Then relax.

End with the thigh muscles, the buttocks, calves, and feet. Extend your feet and toes; point your toes upward to tense the calves and ankles. Hold that posture. Relax. Now bend your toes and tense your calves, your thighs, and buttocks. Relax. Take all the time you need to do this exercise. Inhale deeply and when you exhale give the following instructions to your mind: "Each time I relax more and more."

To help you relax your mind, imagine that you are on an elevator that goes down farther and farther. You feel more relaxed and experience an inner silence. You feel well and at ease. The feeling of lying down on the bed is like flying on a cloud. All is quiet and silent; you are about to fall asleep. Imagine that you are lying on a beach, listening to the waves, or lying on a prairie watching how the clouds move in the sky. Count slowly backwards from fifteen to one, or wait ten seconds between each number knowing that when you reach one you will be completely relaxed.

When you are ready to abandon this state of total relaxation, take three deep breaths and feel how they penetrate your body, invigorating it with new energy. This ritual helps you abandon the mundane world and experience your true divine nature.

Erotic Dance Rituals

Dance is a basic impulse to communicate and express ourselves and it existed much earlier than speech. Dance connects us with nature. Animals dance with specific purposes such as mating, sending warnings when there is a threat, signaling the presence of prey, or in territorial fights. These dances possess choreography and code systems that have been transmitted through hundreds and hundreds of generations.

Dance, for the primitive man, was a tribal activity, very spontaneous and usually with a magic purpose. Everything incites us to dance: weddings, births, deaths, harvests.

The collective consciousness of human beings accesses ecstasy through dance. The psyche seems to follow the rhythm of the cosmos where mysterious and occult energies of the unconscious live. When we dance, we can access the sacred, even though dance is fundamentally erotic. Dance has magical effects and offers sexual power without limits.

During the Neolithic period, people danced in the fields during the harvests to promote fertility by awakening feminine sexual forces. As part of those rituals, some tribes included sexual acts or collective sexual practices. In many cultures, dance was used to honor the gods, the ancestors, or to perform magical ritual, and can lead to states of trance or forms of altered consciousness. In some tribes, shamans may dance in a state of trance to cure someone emotionally or physically.

The Bible mentions religious ceremonies that featured certain types of dances, although there was a time in which the Church considered them immoral. Today old religious rituals inspire dance as performance art.

Dance not only offers physical pleasure, it helps us to express feelings and ideas. Spoken language remains in the illusory or symbolic domain; words can obscure deep truths that are only known to the body and its instincts. Through dance, people of all ages can reconnect themselves to their instincts. Dance may comprise a pre-established vocabulary as in ballet, or may use symbolic gestures to portray certain actions as in mime

—that is, without speech—or only through corporal language as in China and Japan.

Dance is not only an art; it can also be part of a social rite of passage such as a birth, initiation, graduation, or marriage. Today dance offers us a strong reason to bring people together.

How to Perform an Erotic Dance

Dance consists of rhythmical body movements that follow a pattern—usually accompanied by music—that constitutes a form of commun-ication or expression. Erotic dance is the transformation of normal gestures and common expressions into movements that are out of the ordinary, with the goal of enhancing the couple's relationship.

The couple may choose a special time or place to dance with eroticism. The dance ritual used by the couple will be designed by them, although we recommend drawing on Eastern dance forms since they are enormously erotic by nature. In India, some people dance with their eyes closed; this technique may be helpful for those who feel inhibited. Costumes also increase the erotic and physical possibilities: sensual fabrics such as tulle and silk, slippers, special make-up, drawings or tattoos with special inks. All these elements are visually attractive, increase eroticism, and improve the dance.

Ritual with Mantras

The mantra is one of the pillars of a magic union. It is the blend of two words from Sanskrit, an ancient Indian language—MAN: think; and TRA: free.

Mantra signifies unique sound, true sound; it has a special tune as we pronounce it holding our tongue against the upper palate. We do not need to understand the language of the mantras. Just the pronunciation of the word creates the desired effect. When we sing a mantra, it creates vibrations like a church bell ringing and the sound produces light as it is pronounced. This is the sound used to develop "yoga of the mind" or the union of the human mind with the universe in its totality. The singing of mantras elevates the consciousness of the lovers before they perform a magical sexual act.

The most familiar mantra is "OM." OM is the most important mystic syllable from which all other mantras derive. It is the affirmation of the unity of the energy that created the universe and all existence, the consciousness of all living beings, the unity of all powers and attributes of manifest, immanifest, and transcendental beings. OM must not be translated. This mantra represents all sounds that connect a person with universal and supreme dimensions. Use of this mantra is extremely important in developing great compassion and love in a universal sense. Mantras may be used in three different ways:

1. Through singing.
2. Through visualizations or readings without considering the rhythm as it is being sung.
3. Through internal reciting as if someone were whispering in your ear.

It is important to understand that this ritual is a purification that will help us connect with our inner divinity, which manifests through the surrender of our body to achieve the evolution of our soul.

The mantras should be repeated for twenty minutes in the form chosen, whether recitation, singing, visualization, or internal recitation in your mind. This is the time needed for the mind to find its deep silence, without any emotions, memories, or thoughts that cannot be controlled. Through that inner silence we achieve depth.

The following mantra is recommended for a magical union:

OM OM OM NAM, GURU DEV NAMO

As we repeat this phrase our mind is freed from the emotions or images that each lover brings to the sexual union. This mantra must be repeated for about ten minutes. It is very strong when it is recited in unison by the couple and they can hear the rhythm it produces. It is better to recite OM three times first.

Rituals Using Natural Energy
Full Moon Ritual
The moon has feminine qualities; it controls intuition, emotions, and spirituality. It represents the answer to life and to our states of mind.

Since it is associated with the energy of water by its influence on the tides, it governs changes, movements, and rhythms such as pregnancies and physical changes in life. The energy of the moon influences our breasts, ovaries, and digestive system. The full moon every month intensifies our energies and increases our spiritual activity.

Preparations

Find a spot within your sacred space where you and your magical lover can watch the sky and the full moon. Light three white candles on the sacred altar and turn off the lights. Listen to some relaxing music that inspires mysticism, mystery, and spiritual harmony. Practice inhaling and exhaling together as a couple.

To obtain a deeper relaxation, you could move gently to the sound of the soft music. When you feel all your muscles loosen and you are well relaxed, you are ready to start.

Look at the full moon for a few minutes, paying attention to your thoughts and feelings. Then close your eyes and visualize the image of the moon. Imagine a silver light trail that streams from the moon toward you and your lover. The light penetrates your head and then spreads throughout the rest of the body, causing it to glow.

Once you feel that the energy of the moon has permeated your bodies, visualize that the moon's white light has now turned into a wide spiral that covers and protects your sacred space. As you reach the end of your meditation, thank the moon for its power and love and for the special moment it has let you experience. Now take three deep breaths and open your eyes slowly. Look at the full moon again and repeat the thanks. At this time, you can ask for a wish or a request to be fulfilled during this month.

This ritual must be performed before initiating the erotic magic and it may be repeated during the three days of full moon each month. This is a good period for creativity and romantic dates as our bodies tend to change and get more excited at this time.

Cleansing Ritual with Flowers

Water has innate cleansing properties. Since antiquity, it has been used in spiritual ceremonies and it has been associated with the mysteries of our human existence. Water cleanses and purifies negative, stale energy, and it restores lost peace and clarity.

In all corners of the planet we find legends based on the belief that water gives us life, youth, wisdom, and immortality. For Egyptians of the ancient world, it was the source of the origin of the gods. Hindus believe that water is the beginning and end of all things on Earth. In Mesopotamia, water represented the inexhaustible fountain of human wisdom. Many cultures worshiped water because they believed that its sounds and movements represented the soul of a living spirit.

Water is excellent for eliminating negative emotions in a room, person, or object because this element connects us with the plane of feelings. Each time we take a bath we release negative energy and incorporate positive energy in our body. Often we are not conscious of this process, but during this stage of preparation we need to be aware of it. In a magical erotic relationship, the couple may perform together an energetic cleansing ceremony with flowers. This is an ideal way of starting an erotic encounter after a day full of everyday conflicts.

Preparations

Fill a container with previously boiled warm water. Collect red and white petals and place them in the container, and wait till the water reaches an agreeable temperature. Use the water to cleanse the body. To finish, take a regular shower, if desired.

Now the couple is ready to perform any erotic magical act they wish.

Purification Ritual with Sunlight or Moonlight Water and Plants

As we explained in the cleansing ritual with flowers, it is very important to use water to perform different cleansing or purification rituals for the body before performing an erotic act. In this case, we will use the energy of the moon, the sun, and the plants that are suitable for the magical erotic act.

Sunlight Water

The sun is the fountain of life and the origin of all forms of energy that people have used since the beginnings of history. The sun can satisfy all our needs if we learn how to take advantage of its energy in a magical way. It symbolizes all that is creative, individual, and positive.

Fill a container with water and let it stand under the sun to absorb its energy. Usually, three hours is enough to charge the water. This liquid will give you a magnetic, luminous, and expanding energy.

Moonlight Water

The functions of the energy from the moon have already been mentioned in the full moon ritual. Place a container with water under the crescent or full moon for a whole night. You can use that water later on for a cleansing ritual as you did with the water with flowers. You will notice how the energy is soothing for the skin and how tender feelings start to manifest in the magical couple each time they use this water charged with the energy of the moon.

Power Plants

The use of power plants in magic has its roots in time immemorial. The first instances of the use of plant energies occured in rituals using plants and herbs with attributed magical properties. Magic that uses the vegetal world as a tool is called green magic and it is a central element in the practices of the Druids, among others.

To select the plants that best suit your needs, consider the following list:

Almond tree: Only for men. It promotes finding a good love and encourages stability in a relationship without affecting free will.

Blackthorn: Brings good luck and protection.

Cedar: Clears spiritual energies. Eliminates energy blockages caused by bad vibrations or negativity from third persons.

Fir: Its leaves, either fresh or dried, are said to promote fertility. To be more effective, they should be harvested by the person who needs them.

Lemon verbena: Eliminates stale energies that remain in the environment after a discussion. Creates proper spaces for intellectual work.

Lily: Only for women. Its energies can help you find a good love or establish a lasting relationship.

Orange blossom: Its energy is ideal for endless passionate nights since it favors relaxation.

Pine: Clears dense energies, opens new paths. The branches are ideal to stimulate feelings of freedom and action.

Rosemary: The star of love and eroticism.

Charging the Water for a Purification Process

We have to charge the water that will be used in a purification ritual with plants so that it is more than just plain water for a physical cleaning. After deciding which plant to use, determine which type of energy you will need. If you want the water to have strength, you have to use the influence of the sun. If you want to the water to promote serenity, you need the energy of the moon. Proceed with charging the water as discussed above.

Next we will talk about some other magical uses for plants.

Magical Recipes for Love

The magical properties of plants and flowers have been used throughout history in infusions made with water or oils. You can create an infusion by placing the chosen plant in a container with boiling water and letting it cool and sit till part of it evaporates to obtain a pure essence. You can use flower petals, dried fruit skins, and all types of plants. Infused oils can be spread easily over the skin for a massage, improving the well-being of the mind and body, at the same time offering all the magical benefits of the plants used.

The following are some of the essences you could use according to your magical purpose:

Anise: Also a stimulant, but its main benefit is its taste. In addition to using your hands, use your tongue; the pleasure will be better shared.

Basil: Stimulant herb that multiplies its effect when used in oil.

Cinnamon: This is another erotic substance that offers more pleasure if we use the tongue to take advantage of its qualities. Spreading the body with cinnamon essence and licking it all over is a delicious experience.

Clove: A powerful oil that may help prevent early ejaculation. Do not over-use; one drop is plenty.

Geranium: Improves fertility as well as being a magnificent firming oil. You can apply it on the area you would like to treat (for example, the chest, thighs, and abdomen).

Lemon: Use just a few drops to soothe headaches.

Marjoram: Good to calm extreme passion. If your partner is too passionate and you would like to move more slowly, use a few drops of this oil. Use sparingly since in excess it may stop all passion.

Melissa: Good for erotic massages. It is said to prepare the body for a more satisfying love encounter. Improves hormonal irregularities.

Mint: A stimulant as well as being delicious. When applying it for a massage, we can use many of our senses such as smell, touch, and taste.

Orange blossom: For nights of continuous passion since it favors relaxation.

Rosemary: A fragrant and powerful aphrodisiac that helps relieve fatigue. Can also fight rheumatism and help increase blood pressure.

Salvia: A beneficial essence for females, especially if they are in or approaching menopause. Improves the skin, helps fade wrinkles and brings back the spirit of youth.

Sandalwood: The best property is its aroma.

Savory: Aphrodisiac oil that fights mental and sexual fatigue. After a tedious day at work, a few drops of savory and a few caresses are the perfect recipe.

Thyme: A stimulant essence that fights fatigue. Use it when your partner comes home from work very tired.

Ylang-ylang: This is the best aphrodisiac. With a simple massage and some caressing you will give your partner enormous pleasure.

Experimenting with these suggestions may bring pleasure, but never close the door to improvisation. Do some research, learn about herb suppliers and natural-health shops, and ask your partner to share his or her favorites. Thus you will add to and improve the list and adjust it to your preferences.

Base or carrier oils are extremely potent and penetrating. The following oil bases help lubricate and aid erotic massaging:

Almond oil, sweet: One of the best base oils, it can be blended with other essential oils. Smooth, almost without any smell and full of nutrition, it is an antioxidant and contains vitamin E, which is good for the skin. It also has a long shelf life.

Olive oil: Not a good lubricant on its own; must be blended with another base oil. It has a strong smell and special healing properties.

Sesame oil: It must be raw, and must be blended with another base oil since it is not very lubricant. It contains vitamin E and has healing properties for rheumatism.

Soy oil: Has nutritional value and is easy to absorb.

Sunflower oil: Contains a wide variety of vitamins and minerals and it is easy to absorb.

Wheat germ oil: Very dense, with a strong smell and plenty of vitamin E. Recommended for skin conditions, burns, and to retain its properties for a longer time.

Rituals with Erotic Massages and Aromatic Oils

Massage, probably one of the oldest forms of medicine, has been used since the old times in the search for health. There is no doubt that a good massage is extremely enjoyable. To the traditional practice of healing touch, we add oils, essences, and creams to make the experience even more pleasing. A massage promotes mental and physical relaxation, increasing our energy. It is a more elaborate form of the natural instinct to rub the area of the body where we feel pain.

Besides aiding relaxation, a good massage will improve the function of the lymphatic system, promote good circulation, help eliminate toxins, and soothe muscular pain. Our body is an electromagnetic field, and as we receive the massage, our hands become electrical poles. Through that special power of human touch, we experience a new energetic balance at all levels.

When we give or receive massages we become more conscious of the vital energy that dominates our sexuality and magic. The first caresses you give to your magical partner should begin on the extremities. We recommend not touching the genitals at this moment, because sometimes that produces a sexual inhibition. Begin gradually by massaging each other's hands, wrists, feet, and ankles. Later on continue with the arms and shoulders till you get to the chest. Continue with the legs and thighs till you reach the abdomen. These routes represent the main meridians of our energy.

These massages can be very stimulating, especially when we use an oil or moisturizing cream in the erotic areas before the sexual encounter. Any type of sexual caressing, including kisses, activates our endocrine system, favoring the reproductive organs and the production of hormones.

Magic Fingers

There are ten golden rules to performing more effective massages that will make your magical partner explode with passion:

1. Turn this massage technique into a routine. Explore your partner's body for about ten minutes before intercourse. Relax while freeing yourself from all the worries of the day. Use the relaxation ritual technique.

2. When you are done with your relaxation, softly caress your partner's body using some relaxing oil or invigorating cream.

3. Connect with your partner using your hands, voice, and eyes, saying affectionate words that stimulate an emotional reaction or singing a mantra.

4. Synchronize your breathing, especially if you massage each other at the same time so that your circulation works in unison.

5. Start to massage the soles of your partner's feet, and slowly, with a smooth pressure on the sides of the legs, work toward the center of the legs. Always use an ascending movement.

6. For the woman, it is important to touch the clitoris and the lips of the vagina. The stimulus with the fingers may be soft but direct. For the man, use a slight friction while working your way up the legs through the thighs till you get to the pelvis, and massage essential oils on and around the testicles. This is an invigorating act that should be done very gently.

7. Our hands must work like energetic radar, focusing on the feeling of pleasure that our partner shows with each movement. When the partner shows signs of enjoyment, focus on that area of the body. It is possible that that point needs to be touched more often during each sexual encounter.

8. Let your fingers advance over the abdomen. Stroke your partner's body in a spiral manner till you reach the pectorals. This is a highly erotic area for both men and women alike. Continue with circular movements on the pectorals, advancing toward the nipples, till they are stimulated directly.

9. If you have not started your sexual foreplay, continue with the erotic massages following the line of the spine, with smooth pressure along each vertebra, till you get to the neck.

10. Activate the area of the ears with a light friction from inside toward the outside, since that is the area where the organs are reflected. Finish with a light massage on the head to tone the scalp.

Use pure essential oils, derived from the trunk of trees, roots, stems, flowers, and resins, for this massage. To inhale their delightful scents, the oils may be placed in a pressure cooker or a container with boiling water. The vapor will spread the perfume throughout the whole house and create a pleasing environment. You can also heat the oil in a special burner.

Truth Ritual

We all know how difficult it is to manage our emotions. The only way we can create harmonious relationships and marvelous opportunities is to know how our feelings work. Everyone has a perception of their own sexual behavior, but the couple may not share the same opinion. Often, during the course of a relationship, the couple establishes certain erotic roles or patterns. As time passes, the relationship ends up feeling routine and the erotic desire is blocked. The following erotic profiles apply to both genders and may be used to identify the blockages that prevent sexual and emotional intimacy.

Discovering the Erotic Profile

Mental Identity

These people have a rational idea about their sexuality, but when it comes to the act, they have very little flexibility. Intercourse must be performed with certain obsessive rituals to achieve orgasm. This produces dissatisfaction, as they function only at the level of thought and they do not feel connected to their body.

Role to modify if you have this type of profile:

1. Connect yourselves with your inner feelings without trying to rationalize them.

2. Trust your partner and surrender, accepting his or her emotional and physical limitations.

3. Resist the tendency to try to control your partner, or to project your own shortcomings onto the other person.

Body Identity

This erotic profile is very common these days, characterized by the male or female who tries to have a perfect body, showing it off with the latest fashions. People with this profile seduce everyone around them but they never feel fulfilled in a sexual relationship as their sexual arousal is limited to being desired or admired because of their body.

Role to modify if you have this type of profile:

1. Change the focus of your energy, which is centered on your body, to the actual need for love.

2. Pay attention to your feelings of rejection, insecurity or acceptance toward your body and personality.

3. Relate emotionally to other people, abandoning the role of the desired sexual object.

Emotional Identity

Many of those who have confused, conflicted relationships tend to live in the realm of their own romantic fantasies without considering reality.

Role to modify if you have this type of profile:

1. Learn to find pleasure in the physical connection with your partner.

2. Do not feed your fantasies without having real information about your partner's feelings.

3. Don't become drawn in by flattery when that person only looks for a superficial relationship or attempts to take advantage of your emotions.

Once a role is identified, it is very important to attempt to modify it. Here are some techniques to do so.

Take a seat in front of each other, and by turn, ask the necessary questions to clarify or evaluate how the erotic and emotional bond is working. When your partner responds, thank him or her for displaying openness and sincerity. You could ask:

What do you expect from our relationship in the future?

Is there a role I have that bothers you?

Do you feel that our sexual relationship is satisfying emotionally?

Do you think that our relationship is healthy and positive?

The pleasure I feel is complete, but is there anything else you need from me?

The responses must be short and in the first person:

"For me, all aspects of the relationship so far have been . . ."

"I would like to have a more intimate relationship. . ."

"I want to feel more complete by . . ."

"I'd like to do this differently. . ."

Continue asking questions till there is nothing else to say about the subject. When you finish, reflect on the aspects you share and those that were most important, moving or surprising. If you perform this ritual frequently, especially after intercourse, you can modify any negative roles in the relationship. You will share a magical communion, sexual drive will increase and you will reach a deep and true intimacy, which no-one and nothing will be able to break.

Repeat these magical techniques and rituals as often as necessary. In a short time, you will notice how the body and the spirit begin to go through a transformation—improving, nourishing, and releasing all the blocks while the relationship improves. The length and frequency of the rituals must be decided by the couple. Whether the ritual is energizing or erotic, the purpose is to create a place where the lovers merge through the sacred experience of sex. A sexual bond is a mysterious combination of energies in several dimensions. For that reason, we recommend that you:

Accept yourself and accept your lover.

Relate to your lover with depth, clarity, love, and understanding so as to enhance the spirit of sex.

I model your body with passionate touches,
creating thus a symphony of pleasure,
and I go on discovering your fantasies
with intelligence,
like a hidden treasure. I want to be your creator
and your author to perfect together
the art of making love.

Mabel Iam

Chapter 2

The Erotic Zones

While learning about the magic of sex, it is very important to become familiar with the anatomy and functioning of the sexual organs and points of ecstasy.

Sexual pleasure is not only limited to the penis of the man or the clitoris of the woman. The human body contains points that produce pleasurable sensations by simply caressing them. These are called erogenous zones. They are not arbitrary points; they are areas of high nerve ending concentration that are especially sensitive when adequately stimulated.

The primary zones are the parts of the body that are most erogenous, that best respond to any kind of sensual touch and are the best route to arrive at sexual excitement. To stimulate these areas is to invite the release of sexual energy: the nipples and the clitoris of the woman, and the penis or the nipples of the man. The secondary zones are the neck, the center of the back, the ears, the throat, the lips, the back side of the legs, and the anus. These parts of the body respond with high levels of pleasure and excitement, although to a lesser degree than the primary zones.

However, the whole human body can be considered to be an erogenous zone and the stimulation of any point can be a source of pleasurable sensation. Everyone possesses an exclusive and unique erogenous map, and it is important to explore the individual body to discover that person's most erogenous parts.

The search for erogenous points may begin on any part of the body: Feet, eyelids, arms, inner thighs, the nape of the neck, the hair, and all the rest of the body surfaces. Contact with and stimulation of the skin is one of the most important components of sexual activity, and it is important to learn to caress it. You don't have to concentrate only on the typical erogenous zones since the skin is comprised of an infinite number of sensitive points.

You should be aware that not all erogenous zone stimulation will be pleasurable. It depends on various factors, like the skill of the lover doing the stimulating, or the predisposition of the recipient. The discovery and exploration of the erogenous zones should be tender, sensual, and thought-out—in other words, deciding ahead of time what parts of the body (if any) are left out of play. In addition, not all nerve endings are the same for everyone; therefore, not all of our erogenous zones have the same level of sensitivity.

Here are some parts of the body that respond with high levels of pleasure:

Head
Scalp massage produces a very pleasurable relaxation, which is recommended at the beginning and at the end of the sexual act. Utilize the thumbs to give your partner soft circular massages. Also massage the temples and the center of the forehead.

Eyes
The eyelids are full of nerve endings that can be easily excited. Kisses, soft licks with the tongue, and soft finger caresses produce pleasant, stimulating sensations.

Ears

Ears are very sensitive parts of the body, and contrary to general belief, men's ears are sometimes even more so than women's. There are two very sensitive parts for both sexes: the earlobe and behind the ear. Try the following technique: introduce the point of the tongue to the inside of the ear and move it in a circle. Afterward, lick the earlobe and trap it between your lips, squeezing it softly. You can repeat these movements and alternate with caresses on the other parts of the ear with the tongue and lips. You can also blow a little bit behind the ear. If these caresses have an added dose of cuddling, affectionate words and soft whispers, they will melt your partner with pleasure.

Mouth

The sensitivity of the lips increases with excitement, making them very receptive to the rubbing and caresses of another's lips and other body parts. The tongue is able to make soft caresses on any part of the body and, for many people, is the vehicle for the most sensual and exciting sexual games.

Neck, Nape of the Neck, and Shoulders

With the hands or the mouth, one can stimulate the zones of special sensitivity, producing pleasant shivers. If your partner is a man, you will have to use more force to produce the sensation since the skin of men's necks is thicker. In addition, lots of men interpret an aggressive mouth as a signal of excitement. The greater the pressure on the masculine neck, the more pleasure and excitement will result. If your partner is a woman, kiss, lick, and caress the neck. Also rub and gently massage her shoulders. Psychologically, the nape of the neck produces a trusting sensation in the person receiving the caresses and tenderness toward the person who is giving.

Breasts

Men's chests respond sexually but with less intensity than women's. Women's breasts are more sensitive and constitute one of the centers of feminine sexual pleasure. Breasts can be stimulated in many ways; they can be caressed and massaged, kissed, licked, and so on. Try this: cover the chest with moist kisses and little licks, up and down. Then blow on the wet surface. The contrast between cold and hot on the chest produces very exciting results for both women and men. A very exciting sexual practice for both partners is to masturbate the man with the woman's breasts, simply by placing his penis between her breasts and squeezing them around the penis while the man makes vertical movements, similar to those made during intercourse.

Nipples are also very sensitive for both men and women. You can blow, suck, softly nibble or pinch the nipples with your lips while lightly licking them with your tongue.

Arms

Soft, manual stimulation of the armpit area and inner forearm is very pleasurable, but always try to avoid tickling your partner. As with the breast area, this requires gentle stimulation. The inside of the elbow is a secondary erogenous zone and is useful to stimulate in combination with other zones, but not independently.

Hands

The hands have more than four thousand nerve endings. Hold your partner's hand over your mouth and run the tip of your tongue over his or her palm. It is a very unusual and exciting sensation. Another way of doing this is to use your finger to "draw" outward extending spiral circles on the palm of your partner's hand. Use your fingertips to trace up and down your partner's fingers and softly caress them. The receptiveness of the fingers' nerves is continually used to sense textures and forms, and this sensitivity provides a very adequate and pleasant means of feeling your partner's body.

Back

At the sides of the spine are a series of nerves that can be very effectively stimulated either manually or orally by making ascending or descending motions. The sacrum bone, where the back meets the buttocks, is a zone that is more sensitive than the rest.

Abdomen

This zone responds very well to soft rubbing and kissing. The area around the navel is very sensitive on women.

For men, the area between the navel and the pubis is full of nerve endings. To stimulate them, trace a vertical line along this area—not only with your hands; use your tongue and lips to lick, suck, and bite. You can also trace a horizontal line across the abdomen, from one hip to the other.

Groin

This area is especially sensitive on men. Trace the groin with your fingers, and do a soft massage from the hip to the interior of the groin muscle. Combine this with kisses on the front and inside of the muscle. With the fingertips, caress the interior of the groin toward the penis until you arrive at the base of the testicles. Then gently press on the perineum, the region between the testicles and the anus, a few times. This technique can be an excellent prelude to oral sex.

Thighs

The inner thigh, where the skin is the softest, is a very sensitive area that can be a source of pleasure if you caress, lick, or kiss it. Also, try rubbing the thighs with a circular motion.

Buttocks

These contain many nerve endings that can be easily stimulated by little slaps or rubs. For women, movements that lift and open work better than those that flatten or close. Once men are excited, you can drive them crazy with passion by hitting, pinching, or massaging their buttocks. If you are making love in the missionary position, softly hit or squeeze the buttocks of your male partner. Caress one of men's favorite points, where the back meets the buttocks, using both hands.

Prostate

This is called the "masculine G-spot" because of the strong sensations that it produces. The only way to arrive at this muscle directly is through the anus, even though it can be stimulated also through the perineum (see below).

Anus

This has great sensitivity for men and for women alike. It can be stimulated best with the fingertips or tongue, using gentle, circular motions.

Perineum

This is the area between the genital organs and the anus. It is very sensitive to stimulation, although many people do not usually take advantage of the enjoyment it can give them. In the case of women, this zone reacts very well to pressure using the fingertips or circular caresses. In the case of men, it is even more sensitive because under the skin is the prostate, the so-called masculine G-spot. Firmly press with one or two fingers on the skin behind the scrotum. Don't do it for more than a second. Repeat this a few times. The combination of perineum stimulation and oral sex renders extremely pleasurable results.

Feet

The feet are full of nerve endings that can provide very pleasurable sensations, but whatever you do to the feet, make sure not to tickle your partner. You can give soft massages on the soles of the feet, beginning with the heel and moving toward the toes. Pull and massage each toe. Finish by massaging the arch of the foot. Apart from the massage, you can try more sexual games, like little bites, for example. One sexual game that can be very satisfactory for the two of you is to use the feet to play with the genitals of the other partner. Be very careful, though, because we don't have as much control over our feet as we do our hands.

Since the genital organs of both sexes have more sensitive nerve endings, the stimulation of these areas produces the most potent sexual sensations.

The Female Genital Organs

The female external genital system is made up of the mons veneris, the outer lips, the inner lips, the urethral opening, the clitoris and the vaginal opening.

The mons veneris is an area of fatty tissue that covers the pubic bone, and is covered by pubic hair. It has nerve endings that, when stimulated, can provide sexual excitement. The outer lips are vertical pleats of skin.

When not sexually aroused, they are together, protecting the inner lips, the vagina, and the urethral opening. The inner lips are located at each side of the vaginal opening and unite just below the clitoris. They are rich in blood vessels, and they change color and retract during sexual response.

The structure of the clitoris is similar to that of the penis, except that the clitoris is smaller and does not have a urethra. It is located above the inner lips where the lips come together. The clitoris is comprised of a body and a head, or glans. This last part is exposed and has the most nerve endings, making it the area that has the most sexual excitability. During sexual stimulation, the clitoris retracts above the clitoral hood (a skin covering similar to the inner lips) and enlarges.

The clitoris is the most sexually sensitive part of women's bodies and easiest to stimulate. This should be done gently and without haste, so that the area is not irritated. Avoid touching it if it's dry. Before stimulating it, you can lubricate the clitoris by applying saliva with your fingers. Stimulation of the clitoris with the tip of the male partner's erect penis is an extremely pleasurable sensation for many women.

The internal genital system is comprised of the vagina, the cervix, the uterus, the fallopian tubes, and the ovaries.

The vagina is a tubular muscle, capable of dilating considerably, and is approximately four inches long. From the opening to one-third of the way up the vagina is very sensitive, while the rest has only pressure receptors and therefore is not very sensitive. Vaginal lubrication is produced by the vagina during sexual stimulation. This fluid permits easy and painless entrance and facilitates movement of the penis during intercourse.

The entrance of the vagina is rich with nerve endings and reacts intensely to all kinds of touches. The inner lips of the vagina are a lot more sensitive than the outer ones, especially along the interior surface. On the frontal wall of the vagina is something known as the G-spot, which is very sensitive to erotic stimulation. A fun sex game that all women can practice by themselves or with a partner is to find the exact location of the G-spot.

The cervix is the part of the uterus that projects into the vagina. The uterus is a hollow organ with fatty muscular walls. It is pear-shaped and occupies the pelvic cavity. The two ovarian tubes enter at an angle from above the uterus, and lead to the ovaries.

Surrounding the internal genitals are the pelvic muscles. These muscles form part of the lower pelvis and contract during intercourse. There are three different groups of pelvic muscles; the most important ones are the pubococcygeus, which surround the vagina.

The Masculine Genital Organs

The external genitals are the penis and the scrotum. The body of the penis contains three cylinders of erectile tissue: two cavernous bodies, parallel with each other; and the spongy body situated below them that contains the urethra. During sexual stimulation, the erectile tissue fills with blood, making the penis become hard and erect. For an adult male, the average penis length when not erect is two and a half to four inches, with a diameter of a little more than four-fifths of an inch. In its erect state, the penis extends to five to seven inches in length and one and a half inches in diameter. There is a great deal of variation in penis size.

The glans is the head of the penis. In uncircumcised men, it is covered by a pleat of skin, called the foreskin, which is connected to the glans by a band of tissue situated on the upper surface, called the fraenum. It possesses numerous nerve endings and can become irritated if overly manipulated.

Between the interior genitals is the prostate gland, which lies below the urinary bladder. The mature prostate is continuously active; part of its secretions go into the urine, while the rest constitutes the greater portion of the ejaculations together with the secretion of the semen vesicles. The different canals are tubes in charge of transporting the spermatozoids from the testicles to the prostatic portion of the urethra.

The seminal liquid, or semen, is formed by spermatozoids and secretions of the epididymis, seminal vesicles, prostate gland, and the Cowper's glands. The Cowper's glands secrete an alkaline liquid that lubricates and neutralizes the acidity of the urethra so that the semen can safely and rapidly pass through it. It doesn't usually contain spermatozoids, but some can pass through, which is why pregnancy is possible with penile penetration without ejaculation.

The scrotum is the sack of skin that contains the testicles, and the testicles are responsible for the production of the spermatozoids and the sexual hormones.

Testicles are extremely sensitive. They can be stimulated with the tongue, through small licks, or by manual caresses. One should always be careful not to touch them too roughly or hit them.

The penis is the most sensitive area for men, and this is why that zone receives the most intense and pleasurable sensations. The whole penis is very sensitive, but there are two parts that are more so than others. One is the glans, or head of the penis. The most sensitive part of the head is the tip (the crown) which is covered with nerve endings. The other is the fraenum. Due to the extreme sensitivity of these two parts, the best way to stimulate them is orally since contact with the tongue is much softer than with the hands or fingers. You can softly tap them with the tongue and lick them—making circular motions on top, and alternating vertical and horizontal passes along these sensitive areas. In case you use your fingers, or whatever other body part or object, lubricate these zones extensively so that the contact with them will be soft.

How Can You Find the Magical Erotic Points?

In the context of magic, one should know the laws of nature to be able to manage and apply them in daily life. To know the erogenous points, we should remember that simply to find them anatomically does not guarantee sexual ecstasy. If that were the case, no one would have difficulties with their sex life.

Through the magic of sex, we know that there are influential external and internal physical factors that block sexual enjoyment. When we remember our sexual experiences, we don't always recall exciting images from our memory archives. These "mental postcards" generate distinct emotions, from frustration to impotency, but they especially provoke an instinctive fear of repeating a sexual experience that was not very satisfying.

Recent scientific studies have discovered "cerebral maps" that organize acquired knowledge. By means of these mental planes, we are capable of consciously replacing undesired memories with other, more pleasurable, moments. To return to feeling pleasure—without associating the new sexual experiences with the bad memories—it is necessary to develop sexual magic.

Like the way the cerebral organizers function, we can create "sexual maps"—new pleasure routes that directly connect with the senses that we use in the sexual act. The objective is to modify the negative information and delineate new and more positive erotic maps. There are lots of ways to do this, but the simplest is to combine visualization, logic, and emotional memory.

To find and organize the sexual maps and the feelings they provoke, we suggest practicing the following exercise:

1. Take a photo showing the whole body.

2. Photocopy it (enlarge it if it is small) and then attach it to a piece of white paper.

3. Mark each place on the body that provokes some kind of feeling, positive or negative. Use a specific color to indicate each of the two kinds of feelings.

4. After marking the zones, write the name of an emotion according to the pleasure or displeasure that it provokes. When you indicate a part of the body, do it with an arrow or a symbol, like they do on road maps, writing the feeling provoked by stimulation of that place, for example, "delight and passion."

5. For women's bodies, the most sensitive zones are the breasts, more precisely, the nipples, which are primary in reaction to sexual stimulation. Other important feminine erogenous zones are the mons veneris, vaginal opening, anal region, and clitoris (the organ of pleasure *par excellence*).

6. In men's bodies, the erogenous zones are located in the pelvis— the testicles, the penis—but men also feel pleasure in other areas, like the mouth or the neck. The important thing is to create the maps in a conscious way and check out the responses when practicing sexual acts.

7. In the future, we can return to our erotic map to add new associations with physical zones and emotions.

Visualize the magical erogenous zones with concrete feelings (and put them in words), make a conscious change in your memory maps, and connect your sexual being with the divine.

Your body envelopes me, your words fascinate me
like the spell of love. I am so vulnerable
to your look that the further I am from you,
the stronger the magnetism that exerts
your presence inside of my being.

Mabel Jam

Chapter 3

The Magical Senses of Sex

When a person touches someone else's body, the brain receives stimuli from more than five hundred thousand detectors that codify all information about the object being caressed. In a sexual relationship, the body is stimulated completely. How can we take erotic advantage of all that information? During sexual contact, concentration helps us to recognize the infinite and subtle textures of the body. There will be unexplored spaces that may feel soft, rough, flexible, wet, cold, warm, firm, delicate, thin, and thick. It is very important to activate all our senses to enjoy sex in a creative, concrete manner. We will explain in detail the function of all five senses to explore sex with intelligence, and we will show you some erotic exercises to develop those senses in a magical way.

Touch

This is probably the most-used sense during a sexual encounter. However, there is a difference between normal touching and the development of touching as a sense. Many people could take advantage of this suggestion: exercise your sense of touch without aiming at a complete sexual encounter. (See erotic massage rituals in chapter 1.) This is a delicate form of expression useful in finding out what a person likes or prefers.

Usually couples limit themselves to simple, fast, superficial, and stereotypical caressing. As they repeat the same patterns, the contact begins to feel monotonous, eventually leading to lack of interest.

The richer the erotic exploration of both partners, using the five senses, the wider and farther-reaching the language of love will be. A sexual relationship needs a wider language to reach harmony. This sexual harmony, in everyday life, holds the key to the salvation of the couple's relationship, and the key to preventing the decline of sexual intimacy.

Exercise: Blind Touching

To stimulate the sense of touch, before making love, the partners can do the following exercise: Take a handkerchief and use it to cover your eyes to place all the attention on your physical sensations. This exercise can also emphasize the sense of hearing.

Taste

Another sense that is atrophied and that is worth developing if you wish to reach an integral human experience of sexuality as a couple is the sense of taste—a foundation of eroticism.

Kissing is a source of erotic attraction and pleasure in our Western culture. A kiss is probably the most known, cultivated, and accepted form of caressing. As we recognize each sensation, we can generate more pleasure, satisfaction, or ecstasy during the sexual encounter. Our body emanates different flavors during a kiss. We should emphasize the need for proper hygiene so that the pleasure of the kiss is not diminished or lost. But a kiss on the mouth is only an example. The sense of touch combines with the taste of our skin all over our bodies.

Our childhood conditioning plays an important role in the tastes we find pleasant. Nature offers objects for all tastes, and what may be very pleasing for one couple may not be as interesting to another. Mouth-to-genital contact is, from an objective point of view, neither indecent nor an aberration. It can be a demonstration of love and caring, but there is no reason to criticize the omission of such contact when a couple, who has made that decision, can have also a pleasing and otherwise rich erotic relationship.

Savoring the Taste

There are about ten thousand taste buds which help us discriminate among different flavors. How do they work?

Taste buds are located on the tongue. Sour flavors are registered on the sides of the tongue, bitter flavors on the back of the tongue, salty flavors on the top and sweet flavors are well centered at the tip of the tongue. It can be beneficial to introduce some foods that are both delicious and aphrodisiac during the sexual act.

Smell

There is a curious fact about the sense of smell and the dullness of its erotic capacity in our culture. As we do not cultivate this sense, we are susceptible to being exploited by commercial advertising. Cosmetics and pharmaceutical products obscure many natural smells that, if cultivated and recognized, would be as pleasing as the commercial products which we use. The human odor—body smell—may produce either attraction or rejection. We know that this sense of smell is essential for sexual activity in animals. It is a specific odor that attracts the male to the female, and vice versa, during the time of heat.

Apart from this consideration, what we find true among people is that the characteristics of the odor make it attractive. The smell of the body and of the sexual organs arouses and stimulates eroticism. In spite of all subjective elements and childhood conditioning, smells have inspired lyrics and poetry.

Exercise: Develop the Senses of Smell and Touch

Place in water the petals of a flower, such as jasmine or a rose, and wait until they impart their fragrance to create a sensual perfume. Bathe your hands in this fragrant liquid and with that aroma impregnated in your skin, you can touch your partner to take him or her to a state of rapture. Using the flower ritual explained in chapter 1, perhaps, can become an exercise in this sense.

Sight

Sight may be the primary sense used by humans, and visual stimulation is an important part of eroticism. What does the man see in the woman and the woman in the man? Some try to negate the visual and perceptible characteristics of sight in a human erotic relationship. We know, however, that that is not true. It is evident that the manifestation of what the senses sense and experience does not necessary match the rules of what we call "correct norms of society." These norms have atrophied the great erotic potential of visual perception.

The sensuality of people deprived of vision is different compared to the people with sight. This is a reality. We can caress with our eyes, and that should be cultivated to promote magical and erotic chemistry. Seeing and looking at each other allows us to share admiration of and appreciation for our partner.

Cultural patterns and customs tell us that men have developed the more erotic visual faculty compared to women. Common sense tells us that a woman, like a man, likes to see the person she loves. But making love in a darkened room is a widespread element of social conditioning. Without going into many arguments, think about this common saying: out of sight, out of mind. Why would sexuality be different?

Hearing

The sense of hearing is an erotic antenna, especially for women, much as sight is for men. The ear is receptive to spoken words and sounds, and some sounds are gestures of sensuality, such as music. We all know the power of seduction that Don Juan exercised through his words, and if he seduced women, it was because they all fell for his words.

Other people find that silence is more pleasing. In general, men do not talk much during sexual intercourse. A woman, on the contrary, feels the need to express herself. Just before climaxing a woman might emit groans or moans, lyrical expressions, or impassioned interjections. A woman needs more words from her partner, although he may not, in his own excitement, be able to express himself. "Love words" during an intimate encounter are the result of feelings and, at the same time, they excite our senses. Sometimes there is even the need to express the excitement in other ways, with common expressions, even crude ones, or humorous phrases or with the special, intimate language developed by the couple.

Exercise: Develop Our Five Senses

When the couple stops their love play briefly before changing position, they could eat some food with stimulating flavors. They can eat, observe or taste, paying attention to the sounds and flavors in their mouths. Even more so, if the food is applied to the body, a new, stimulating sensation arises. The food could be honey, cream, chocolate, sparkling wine, and, especially, aphrodisiacs. What is important is the sharing.

An aphrodisiac is any substance believed to increase sexual appetite. The name refers to Aphrodite, the Greek goddess of love, who was born from the sea when the god Kronos killed and castrated her father, throwing his genitals into the water. Some aphrodisiacs stimulate other senses as well—sight, touch, smell and hearing—and others are taken as food, beverages, alcoholic drinks, "love philters" or potions, drugs, or medical preparations. In ancient Indian texts, we find a variety of ways men can increase their sexual vigor with foods such as milk or honey, which have always been recognized as sources of energy. Traditional Chinese medicine uses herbs as a base for medications, such as ginseng to increase longevity and sexual drive. The Arabs emphasized the value of perfumes, fragrances, and cosmetics to multiply sexual pleasure. Among the Saxons, plants with a phallic appearance, such as carrots and asparagus, were popular.

Modern science today recognizes only a small number of aphrodisiacs. One of them is cantharides—commonly known as Spanish fly—which consists of dried and minced insect parts. You must be very careful if using it, since it is an extremely dangerous stimulant for human beings due to its high toxicity. Here are some other examples of aphrodisiacs:

Alholva: Sold in herbalist's shops, the grains are ground to powder. Boil two tablespoons per cup of water. You can add honey to taste.

Ambergris: The best way to use ambergris is to crush it with sugar and mix with a hot beverage such as chocolate or tea. (Do not confuse it with yellow amber, which is a mineral.)

Brains: All dishes containing brains may be considered aphrodisiac due to the phosphoric content.

Celery: Contains an aphrodisiac natural substance called comarina, which stimulates blood circulation, and can be eaten either raw or as part of a cooked dish.

Cinnamon: Apart from its universally known aphrodisiac properties, cinnamon is also an antiseptic and aids digestion. The cooked bark is used usually as a powder. Boil 15 milligrams of cinnamon in four cups of water.

Clove: Besides its aphrodisiac properties, it is also an antiseptic.

Coriander: A plant known for its aphrodisiac properties. Can be used in infusions with 25 grams per liter of water, or you can drink the Vasc liqueur called Izarra which contains coriander.

Eggs: All types of eggs are said to be aphrodisiac, especially quail.

Ginseng: A potent aphrodisiac and stimulant for all the body. Use the roots, which you can find in health food stores as pills, powder, tinctures, and so on.

Invigorating herbs: Herbal mixtures of ginseng, royal jelly, guarana, ginko biloba, and pollen.

Hoang-nan: This potent aphrodisiac is toxic in large amounts. Usually sold in five-gram tea bags.

Kola: It is a nervous system stimulant, but its aphrodisiac properties have not been proven.

Mint, seasoned: Seasoned mint has a double action; it is soothing for the nervous system as well as being a stimulant of the genital organs.

Nuoc-mam: Exotic condiment known for its exceptional aphrodisiac properties.

Nutmeg: Mix some nutmeg into juices or cocktails; it slows down ejaculation.

Nettle, stinging: This is a good remedy for impotency. Take a teaspoon of stinging nettle every day, mixed with a tablespoon of honey.

Peppers: An aphrodisiac that will also cleanse your intestines.

Rosemary: A well-known aphrodisiac with invigorating properties for the heart, especially for weakness and palpitations. Make an infusion with two soup spoons of rosemary to four cups of water.

Snails: Most crustaceans and mollusks are believed to have aphrodisiac properties.

Thyme: Excellent stimulant for the psyche in general. Drink an infusion made with one teaspoon to four cups of water.

Truffles: They are a potent, but expensive, aphrodisiac.

Ylang-Ylang: The essence of an aphrodisiac plant used in perfumes.

By using our creativity and the erotic intelligence of our senses in each sexual act we can take advantage of the full capacity of our brain, and become a genius in the art of lovemaking. But before dealing with the deep senses that are related to sexual magic, in the form of magnetism, we have to review how the five senses influence the art of caressing and seducing.

To caress is not only to touch and feel. It is also to look, to see, to smell, to listen, and to taste. All our senses take part in this work of art, the same as all colors come together in a masterpiece. A caress is the most integral and complete gesture that a man and a woman can use to express their feelings as a couple. Caresses and seduction are a specialty, and we know all too well that this art is sometimes forgotten.

Suggestion and Autosuggestion

One of the most important aspects in understanding sexual magic is to know, develop, increase and manage the deep senses related to the art of erotic magnetism. This is made possible by tapping into the subconscious mind.

The power of suggestion, similar to hypnosis or self-hypnosis, is a psychological process that, when controlled, can lead to a person accepting direction by another person. Each idea understood by the brain tends to be translated as an act.

Is it possible to use suggestion in dialogues with oneself or others? Yes, but to achieve results, one must have complete faith in oneself. A person is what he or she thinks. That is why we must think carefully about the idea—and the sexual content of the idea—that we wish to convey.

Suggestion may also be defined as an affirmation intended to strengthen an idea about oneself or others. By using the untapped potential of the mind, it is possible to have thoughts full of strength, greatness, and power. If we exercise that power, gradually we will begin to display the desired traits or behaviors to ourselves and around others.

Exercise: Using Suggestion

Practice this exercise every day before getting up or after going to bed, while you feel relaxed. After doing the relaxation and breathing ritual (see chapter 1), repeat to yourself the following: "I trust myself and I have great magnetism in my relationships with others." Or repeat something like this: "I am freeing myself of all my inner conflicts and I am sexually attracting the person I desire."

It is important to repeat this phrase on a regular basis with the absolute certainty that the magnetism we have created will be irresistible to anyone.

Subliminal Seduction

As we mentioned before, the art of seduction is magical. To be a magical or a sacred lover you must recognize and transcend the common messages that produce seduction in all persons.

Subliminal messages have a notorious reputation, as they can be used with a clear intention to manipulate for commercial or political reasons. Much research has been done on subliminal stimuli and perceptions for therapeutic purposes.

Subliminal communication targets the unconscious mind, which does not have the same capacity to evaluate information that the conscious mind does. During the process of subliminal communication, the conscious mind often is not able to detect the messages, except in the case of people with very alert minds or people trained in meditation techniques or creative visualization.

Which mechanism in our minds allows us to perceive certain words and which components of those words make them pleasing or arousing to the recipient? A variety of stimuli in the cerebral cortex comes from the sense organs and, in the case of sexual motivations, they come from two sources: The internal source provides the fantasies, and the senses provide the external source. Both are interpreted by the brain and converted into stimulation or rejection.

Seduction is, no doubt, one of the games most often played by human beings. This game has its own rules and patterns of behavior. Attraction depends on an infinite number of social and cultural factors. In order to achieve an effective subliminal seduction, you must:

1. Control the emotions of the sender while focusing the attention of the receptor on a certain fascinating characteristic

2. Convincingly transmit a seduction message to obtain the approval and liking of the receptor

There are several forms of seduction:

Argumental seduction: The sender makes comments about certain characters which are intended to interest the receptor and cause him or her to identify with those characters.

The seduction of power and fame: People project their own wishes and desires onto politicians, celebrities, athletes, and artists.

Affective seduction: The sender attempts to make the receptor like him or her as a means of gaining influence over the receptor.

Subliminal seduction: The attempt to seduce by influencing the unconscious mind of the receptor.

Seduction through information: Mass media uses information to reach the audience and to persuade them to act.

Magical Strategies to Become a Subliminal Seducer

These guidelines are infallible and when used with creative visualization will turn you into an irresistible subliminal seducer or seductress.

Be unpredictable. Don't fall into patterns of behavior.

Try different strategies according to the moment or the opportunity.

Exercise emotional self-control. Keep your feelings in check even when your body feels the heat.

Use the element of mystery in your conversation and your persona.

Demonstrate indifference. Absence creates expectations.

Be bold and audacious. If you think about it, do it.

Don't say, "May I give you a kiss?" Just give the kiss!

It is better to try it than to feel sorry for not having done so.

Show the person you want to seduce that he or she can count on you. Make your presence indispensable.

Each person has a weak point; try to find it and exploit it. This is the art of moving wills.

Use unexpected surprises, but do not overwhelm the person with presents.

A little bit of romanticism never fails.

Keep your partner in suspense. Do not show all your cards and do not show them all at the same time.

Remember:

A seduction game has infinite rules, as many as the emotions it provokes.

You must always be responsible for all reactions that you generate.

The magnetism and charm promoted by subliminal seduction can be obtained by trying and proving the success of each of the strategies mentioned. Start today. Create your first successful subliminal seduction.

How to Cause Sexual Magnetism

Who has not, at least once, been seduced by the fascination emanating from people with charisma? That magnetic power is related to the hypnotic control of the mind.

Each object, as we know, has its own magnetic field. Human beings have a special active magnetic charge, and the erotic field is one of many that we influence.

All persons have the faculty to project a vital flow of energy. These waves are capable of influencing, even at a distance, those we desire sexually. The magnetic field of one person directly influences another person in a trance state or suggestion situation. But to be able to use that powerful magnetic flow, and to be able to transmit that attraction we have, it is necessary to develop our own suggestive power.

A person may have three types of sexual magnetism:

1. A physiological action called "animal magnetism"

2. A more subtle and hidden action that acts from a distance through will and thoughts

3. A reaction produced by an external characteristic: the resonance of the voice, a special presence, an alluring behavior, a certain look, and other specific gestures

A belief is the feeling of certainty about the meaning of an experience, situation, or emotion. The certainty we have about what is possible helps us reach great objectives. During thousands of years people thought that the Earth was flat; they were certain it was so, even though that concept was later proved to be incorrect.

Deep in one's own self we find established beliefs that limit our sexuality; those beliefs are as incorrect as the old beliefs of our ancestors about the shape of the Earth. No matter how wrong a belief, it can seem written in stone, like Moses' Commandments. The more unconscious or unquestionable a belief is, the more powerful it becomes. If it is positive and invigorating, there is no problem, but if it is negative, it needs to be re-examined.

The experiences we analyzed in the previous exercises create the necessary conditions so that sexual shame does not develop. If we continue learning that something is natural and normal, we develop the belief that it is so.

Erotic Telepathy

Have you ever had an experience in which an unfamiliar situation suddenly seems familiar? How many times have you heard the expression "I know what you are thinking"?

Perhaps we can interpret such situations as the result of a pleasing and effective love relationship, or a deepened, perfect mental communication between two people. But what does the mind communicate and how does that communication function?

We cannot talk about the mind without exploring the functions of the brain. The brain consists of two hemispheres, which are interconnected but have different functions. The left hemisphere controls our rational and analytical thinking, language, and mathematical functions, and it connects us to external reality. The right hemisphere controls the artistic and intuitive aspects; it communicates to our inner reality.

Thus, the mind enables us to receive external sensations which affect our inner reality. The mind has a conscious level which is in direct contact with the cerebral hemispheres and interprets the different realities we perceive.

The mind has an unconscious level that is constantly working beyond the present space and time, controlling all the functions of the body and receiving the energy of the different dimensions of the collective or universal mind. The human organism generates electromagnetic, electrostatic, magnetic, and gravitational energies, all of which are interrelated.

A series of experiments shows that a person may generate communication with another's mind through an as-yet-unidentified cerebral function. This phenomenon is called spontaneous telepathy.

Spontaneous telepathy is produced in an unconscious manner. It has been proven that spontaneous telepathic transmissions are intimately related to the affective union of the two subjects. Those persons attract a certain type of "loving energy" that aids the back-and-forth transmission of thoughts.

Within spontaneous telepathy, there is a variant called "linking energy"—a more random type of contact where there is apparently no previous relationship between the receptor and the sender. The receptor may incorporate this information into his or her unconscious in various ways—dreams, intuition, premonitions, and so on. This explanation may be the key to experiences where a person asks himself or herself, "Have I lived before or dreamed what is going on now?" And the answer may be that it is a piece of information transmitted and revealed by another mind in subconscious contact with one's own.

The Sixth Sense

The Lamas in Tibet believe that minds can enter into contact through a sixth sense that is atrophied, but which can be exercised and put into conscious use.

According to these Eastern beliefs, telepathy is related to our pineal gland. This gland produces the mental energy needed to telepathically contact other people without any need to know them beforehand.

What is most important is to be open to the magic that we encounter every day. The secret is that you have the power to go beyond all that you think you know, and discover by yourself the true and deep perception of what we call reality.

In the next chapter we will explain how the energetic bodies and the centers of energy work. This knowledge will help you use and find out more about erotic magic to widen your spiritual world.

All we experience must be attributed
to our body, and all that exists within us,
all that we can ever conceive, exists in our body
and must be attributed to our soul.

Mabel Jam

Chapter 4

Our Bodies and Their Energy

We have already discussed the physical nature of the body's organs in chapter 2. Now we will learn how the energy centers function. Without this knowledge, we cannot go deeper into the magic of eroticism. Here we will give definitions for interpreting what are commonly referred to as the physical, emotional, and mental bodies.

This explanation will be useful for understanding and working with the different energy levels. You will learn to use and understand the energy of the chakras, including the ability to change, clean, heal, and unblock the human body. In this exploration, we will also discover what impedes us from relating to each other with the fullness that we deserve.

Our Physical Body

The physical body, whether it is mineral, animal, man, or planet, is made up of millions of atoms or cells. Every form possesses a condition of constant activity, and each one preserves its individuality or identity united by a central attractive and coordinating force called life.

One should draw a clear distinction, nevertheless, between man as merely a physical form, and what comprises a complete human being. The difference lies in the duality of the last concept—a human being has a soul that serves as a union between spirit and matter. Even though the physical body has its own life, this only represents biological life and one without consciousness. Without the direction of the soul, the body would be nothing more than an automaton without feeling. The physical body can be thought of as a form responding automatically to the consciousness that unfolds gradually.

Every atom of every form is made up of concentrated energy in various densities. Physical matter, in its multiple states, is the expression of the only essence—energy—existing in the universe.

In synthesis, the cells of the body are molecules of light and energy that act according to different vibrations, under the control of spiritual consciousness that can liberate, transform, and recreate energy.

Our Emotional Body

The variety of emotions we all feel comprises our emotional body, creating a body of matter similar to a body of water surrounding the physical body.

Emotional matter is much more subtle than physical matter. Even though its location is out-of-body, the emotions are clearly translated in people's gestures and behavior. The connection with the physical body is realized through the solar plexus chakra. This is why emotions are "felt" in this zone, often mistakenly associated with the heart or stomach area (later on in this chapter we will explain the function of the solar plexus chakra).

Emotional energies and mental energies generated by thought are different. Certain ways of thinking generate emotions, and the emotional influence generates thoughts.

Created emotions will have the characteristics of strength and endurance, depending upon how we nourish them through our thoughts. The emotional matter of every being is perceptible as a halo of different colors around the physical body; this is what we call the aura. The dominant colors of the aura represent the emotional characteristics of a person and his or her level of evolution. Such perception is realized by means of the chakra of the third eye, the physical organ of intuition, in interaction with the physical eyes.

Our emotions are transmitted very easily and can affect other individuals. That is why, for example, it is easy for one person to have a happy or sad effect on a gathering, according to the emotional form we create. Emotional matter directed through conscious or subconscious thought has the ability to affect concrete matter. That is how powers emanate from cult locations, talismans, and so on.

For a human being in the lower levels of evolution, emotion dominates thinking. In the higher evolutionary levels, the thoughts dominate and control the creation of emotional forms. It is vital to arrive at a clear comprehension of the emotional plane. By understanding its nature, a person can learn to remain free of negative emotional forms—both one's own and those of others.

The emotional body of humans plays the role of the great reflector, and at the same time is a less reliable mirror, always distorting the image that it receives. The body records every kind of force or influence around it, and mixes all of the colors and movements, and every kind of desire, action, and sound into a confusing conglomeration of impressions. The objective of the individual who aspires to achieve sexual magic should be to impose order on this chaos, and calm the agitated surface of the waters of this plane to the point where it can serve as a clear mirror to reflect the qualities and impulses of the soul. Aspiring magicians should liberate their emotional body of all fear and worry, cultivating a sense of serenity and stability, and a feeling of secure dependency in the superior forces. You should work with your negative emotions—envy, depression, greed, or self-pity—and calmly proceed on your path with tranquil and happy confidence in your heart.

Our Mental Body

Mental energy is not located in the brain, but in the mental body, which is even more subtle than the emotional body. It utilizes the brain as an organizer of memories. Through thought, the brain processes mental energy and has its expression in the physical-material realm. This connection is realized through the crown chakra, which is located in the highest part of the brain.

The strength and duration of the mental forms and images created by thought will depend on the intensity and frequency with which they were created, as was explained in the previous chapter about magical telepathy. When compatibility exists, mental forms can be captured by another human being, as in telepathy (if it happens while they are being generated) or clairvoyance (if one accesses a mental image created by the thought of the transmitter). Always, either directly or indirectly, to a lesser or to a greater degree, they cause an effect in other individuals.

Such effects will be positive or negative, according to how they were created and, very especially, will have repercussions on the person who generated them. The congeniality of some people—painters, musicians, poets, scientists—is the result of constancy in their practice of concentration and meditation. This is what gives one the realization of the physical sphere of advanced forms of thought.

The ability to access and process mental matter will vary according to one's evolutionary grade. During the time that is spent doing internal work, the magician or divine lover progresses and evolves constantly. In the first level, all of the energies are focused on the physical body. The next stage progresses to the emotional body. Through this stage, you should become adept at and gradually submit to mental control, until you achieve harmony, peace, love, serenity, and spiritual and emotional stability.

The Chakras

We do not know much about how the powerful energy of life functions, or how we can make the most of it and obtain the most pleasure from our bodies. As was already explained, the mental plane is composed of the energy of one's thoughts and is related to the emotions. The physical plane is the energy related to what surrounds us and what can be received through the senses. The most subtle energy is spiritual energy because it integrates the three planes: physical, emotional, and mental. However, in all of these cases, the energy is transmitted through the chakras.

Chakra means *"center"* in Sanskrit. There are seven energy centers and their function is to concentrate and emit the three energy levels. They are located at different points on the body. The three inferior chakras are in charge of processing emotional energy and the four superior chakras are related to mental energy.

Chakras influence physical activity through the functioning of the glands and their secretions that affect physical functioning, mental movement, and emotional integrity. This is to say, our emotions or thoughts will be constructive or destructive according to how we utilize the energy of the body.

Physical Location of the Three Inferior Chakras

1. At the base of the spine

2. Under the navel

3. At the top of the stomach

Physical Location of the Four Superior Chakras

4. In the heart

5. In the throat

6. In the space between the eyebrows

7. At the top of the head

Each chakra is located in a specific position on the physical body and, at the same time, can work for the liberation of its associated energy in the other planes. Later on, we will describe some exercises for unblocking and working in the three energy levels (mental, physical, and emotional).

This will help you understand how the chakras function and at what level their energies can be harmonized. These exercises will have the effect of improving your personal relationships.

To achieve a true exploration and harmonization of the energy centers, it is important to do these exercises in a sacred place. They should be practiced for twenty minutes at least twice per week to achieve the magical effect and to be able to control your energy. If it is possible to repeat the exercises daily, you will establish a better magical connection with your partner and with the environment. All of the following exercises should be done after the ritual of relaxation and breathing so as to enable the perfect visualization.

The Root Chakra: Vital Energy

Located in the base of the spine, this chakra forms the connection to the Earth and physical matter. It is the place where energy flows with the greatest intensity.

When this center is harmonized, it has the following attributes: Survival instinct, vitality, mental balance, security, confidence, self control, serenity, innocence, and altruism.

Without harmonization: Irrational fears, violence, rage, physical maladies, and psychological despondency.

Related color: White

Exercise: Mental Plane

So that this chakra functions correctly, you should visualize it as a center or wheel of white light at the base of the spine at the level of the anus. White is the color of energy purification.

Exercise: Physical Plane

Walk slowly and, after a few moments, focus on the first chakra, at the base of the spine (you can also try focusing on the feet). Be conscious of what happens to the physical form when you are walking.

Exercise: Emotional Plane

Now, contract and relax the sphincter. What effect does this movement have on the emotional form when you are walking or standing?

The Sexual Chakra: Find True Love

This center is found under the navel. It has influence over the nervous system and body temperature, and is in charge of radiating harmony to the body, mind, and the emotions.

When this center is harmonized, it has the following attributes: Inspiration, creativity, aesthetic qualities, pleasure, intimacy, clarity, sensitivity, amazement, enthusiasm, eroticism, and sexual energy.

Without harmonization: Jealousy, feelings of possessiveness, hysteria, sexual problems and illnesses of the uterus, the prostate, and the bladder.

Related color: Pink.

Exercise: Mental Plane

This center should be visualized with a pink light, in the form of a wheel in the genital area. The pink color is related to the energy of love.

Exercise: Physical Plane

Stand with the legs slightly separated (in line with your shoulders) and the feet forward and parallel, bend a little at the knees to avoid tension in the back of the legs, and align the pelvis. Incline the pelvis forward several times (creating a little arc in the lumbar region) and then backward (curving the back), until you find a rhythm that is comfortable to maintain.

While you inhale and rock the pelvis forward, contract the pubococcygeus (PC) muscle, as if you were retaining urine. When you exhale, rock the pelvis backward and relax the PC muscle. Note how the perineum (the area between the genitals and the anus) relaxes. If you have difficulty noticing the sensations of the perineum, imagine that the genitals inflate. Continue contracting and relaxing the PC muscle as you breathe and maintain the rhythmic movement. Pay attention to the sensations that awake in the pelvis region.

Exercise: Emotional Plane

Focus your attention on the anus in order to move the vital energy of the sexual chakra forward. You can feel a hot sensation and a kind of a tickle in the pelvic region and the genitals. If that is not the case, pay attention to how you feel and continue breathing. Make a circular movement with the pelvis: forward, to the side, behind, to the other side, and so on. Continue until you have a continuous and fluid circle—as in Arab dancing. Pay attention to the area below the navel, in the middle of the lower abdomen, while the energy is being directed from the anus to the genitals.

Try to contract and relax the sphincter and the PC muscle while you swing your hips (the contraction takes place when the pelvis moves forward, and the relaxation happens when the pelvic moves backward). Recognize the quality of movement and the thoughts and images that come to your mind.

Separate the legs a little more and, with the knees slightly bent, shift the weight of the body from one foot to the other and repeat this several times. Are you able to maintain equilibrium? Place your attention on the Hara—the point below the navel, located in the abdomen—and imagine that the energy that helps maintain equilibrium emanates from that point. Continue changing the weight from one foot to the other, but now with one of the feet forward, shift the weight to the back or at an angle. Observe and feel how the vital and sexual energy coming from the genitals is directed to the center of the abdomen. Pay attention to any perceivable difference in how your balance is maintained, and the feeling of internal power.

The Solar Plexus Chakra: Harmonize the Emotions

The solar plexus chakra is located at the top of the stomach, above the navel. It has influence over the digestive system and rules the subconscious. It is related to the fire of our primary emotions.

When this center is harmonized, it has the following attributes: Talents, common sense, will, prudence, determination, success, strength, tolerance, serenity, ability to relate to others, skills, self-esteem, and the ability to laugh.

Without harmonization: Bad digestion, a craving for sugar, fear of not being loved, inability to say no, arrogance, fear of separation, grandiose airs, and feelings of power.

Related color: Violet

Exercise: Mental Plane

Visualize a wheel of violet, the color of transformation, at the top of the stomach. When this center is not functioning properly, it provokes conflicts, jealousy, and the unwillingness to reject that which is damaging.

Exercise: Physical Plane

Stand with your legs slightly spread and in line with your shoulders. Let the thorax extend itself forward when you inhale and toward the back when you exhale. Continue breathing in this manner to amplify the movement in front of and behind the thorax. While you breathe, extend your arms forward and observe the rocking of the thoracic cavity. Bring your partner close to you and rest your hands on his or her solar plexus.

Exercise: Emotional Plane

When noting an emotion, observe how the energy works. Understand how the sexual energy is directed from the base of the spine to the genitals, to the abdomen and from there to the solar plexus. Recognize the sensations, emotions, colors, and images that arise.

The Heart Chakra: Return to the Heart

This energy center is located at the same height as the heart and governs the feelings of compassion and unconditional love. On the mental plane, it permits the ability to comprehend things beyond time and space and is the center of the higher emotions. This chakra is related to divine wisdom, internal stability, patience, mental balance, and suffering and pleasure. When it is activated, the fourth chakra stimulates vitality and cerebral activity, invigorates the glandular system and activates internal secretions. The thymus gland is located above the heart chakra and is responsible for the body's immune system. If the energy in this chakra is blocked, so will be the function of this gland, and the immune system will be suppressed. Its blockage does not permit the normal flow of emotions.

When this center is harmonized, it has the following attributes: Love, security, confidence, objectivity, compassion, forgiveness, respect, transcendence, vitality, patience, acceptance, devotion, perseverance, wisdom, group consciousness, and peace.

Without harmonization: Heart problems, weakness, immune system problems, prejudices, egoism, rigidity, lack of love, spiritual emptiness, emotional problems and imbalances.

Related colors: Pink, blue, yellow

Exercise: Mental Plane

To regulate this center, you should visualize the three colors in the form of one ray of light entwined in the heart area. The color pink is associated with love, blue with power, and yellow with wisdom.

Exercise: Physical Plane

Make yourself comfortable with your eyes closed and with the palms of your hands one on top of the other on your chest. Begin the balancing in a pleasant manner. Imagine or remember a scene in which you have felt profoundly loved. Focus your attention under your hands and observe what happens.

Exercise: Emotional Plane

Think of a loved one and imagine that the love feels likes rays of the sun. Extend your arms, as if sending that love, while maintaining the heart chakra as the focus of your attention. Repeat this action several times—the love flows from the heart chakra outward and then returns to the heart—until it acquires a relaxed and fluid respiratory rhythm. Observe what happens.

The Throat Chakra: The Power of Communication

This center is located in the throat. It has influence over communication, expression, hearing and the development of telepathic capacities. It controls and energizes the throat, the thyroid and parathyroid glands, the lymphatic system, the vocal and bronchial apparatus, the nourishment canal, and internal hearing. It is responsible for rejuvenation and longevity, for the subconscious mind and creativity. When this chakra is stimulated, a person can transform other types of human energy and find unconditional enjoyment as much in the physical plane as in the spiritual.

When this center is harmonized, it has the following attributes: Communication, comprehension, spontaneity, sympathy, diplomacy, rejuvenation, longevity, the capacity to speak and hear the truth, telepathy, the ability to listen through the hearing of another person, personal integrity and consciousness of the subtle world.

Without harmonization: Allergies, fatigue, dizziness, asthma, deafness, loss of voice, confusion, problems communicating with others, and repressed emotions.

Associated color: Blue

Exercise: Mental Plane

Visualize a blue light in the shape of a wheel in the throat area. Blue is the color of divine power that transcends humans.

Exercise: Physical Plane

Find a comfortable position while standing or seated. Relax the jaw and begin to sing the OM mantra. Sing it loudly and passionately, while focusing your attention on the throat chakra and observing what happens.

Exercise: Emotional Plane

Try to direct the vital and sexual energy from the root chakra upward to the throat. As you inhale, perceive, feel, and imagine that all of that energy is liberated through the voice.

The Third Eye: Inner Wisdom

It is from this center, located in the space between the eyebrows, that a person harmonizes his or her strengths and achieves balance between the ying and the yang. Persons with a third eye that is awake can balance their feminine and masculine energies and develop restraint and exquisite feelings. Stimulating this center promotes clairvoyance. Its awakening grants spiritual evolution and dominion over matter. At the physical level, it corresponds to the pituitary gland and the nervous system in general. It controls various planes of reason—intuitive and rational thought, and memory.

When this center is harmonized, it possesses the following attributes: Memory, concentration, rational and intuitive thought, imagination, visualization, devotion, equilibrium between the ying and the yang, clairvoyance, restraint, dignity, forgiveness, mental capability, consciousness without thoughts, dominion of the spirit over matter, capacity to transform physical reality, fusion of the conscious and subconscious minds, evolution and control over one's destiny.

Without harmonization: Headaches, vision problems, sinusitis, mental illnesses, little ability to pay attention and concentrate, memory loss, excessive intellectuality, senile dementia, lack of logic, and fear of the future.

Related color: Emerald green

Exercise: Mental Plane

Visualize this center as a wheel of light, the color emerald green, in the space between the eyebrows. This color is associated with the planet Venus, regent of universal love.

Exercise: Physical Plane

Sit or stand in a comfortable position. Breathe deeply, and while exhaling, let your abdomen become relaxed. While inhaling, imagine that the energy ascends from the base of the spinal column through the genitals, through all of the energy centers, until it arrives at the area between your eyebrows, the third eye. While inhaling, maintain your attention on the third eye. Repeat this exercise several times, adding the contraction and relaxation of the PC muscle.

Exercise: Emotional Plane

Allow your respiration to go to the second plane and fix your attention on the third eye. Be conscious of whatever image, vision, or intuition that emerges while you repeat this process several times.

The Crown Chakra: Illumination

This center is located in the top part of the head and is a receptor for radiant cosmic energy. The person that awakens this chakra has achieved fullness, has transcended fear and can comprehend universal creation without limits. In the Tantra, this last state of stimulation corresponds to the union of the feminine Shakti with the masculine Shiva, which is eternal union with the universe. This chakra controls the brain and promotes happiness and spiritual and physical enjoyment without limits.

When harmonized, it has the following attributes: Inspiration, spirituality, cosmic consciousness, the higher Self, unconditional spiritual enjoyment, integration, evolution, union with the Divine, unlimited ability of creation, transmutation, goodness, universal love, and consciousness of being one with the universe.

Without harmonization: Lack of inspiration and creativity, deep depression, disconnection with physical reality and the spiritual self.

Related color: Golden

Exercise: Mental Plane

Visualize that a golden light penetrates your crown chakra from the center of the universe. This light penetrates all of your body and vibrates with a golden color that corresponds with pure wisdom.

Exercise: Physical Plane

Breathe from the base of the spine to the crown chakra, at the top of the head. Imagine that your breathing emanates from the base of the spine and rises up the spinal column through all of the energy centers, floats for a few moments just above the crown and returns, descending the spinal column.

Exercise: Emotional Plane

While you continue breathing in this way, maintain your focus on the crown chakra. Pay attention to any images or feelings that occur without trying to control them.

Learning to move the energy from the base of the spine to the crown takes some time, but with regular practice, the benefits are immense. Once you have perfected the technique, you will discover that sexual ecstasy will not only be produced in the genital area, but in the whole body. It is, furthermore, an essential element to achieving an ecstatic union with a magical partner and experimenting with universal unity.

When the woman unites with the love of the man,
all the magic power of the universe
is integrated and that act produces miracles,
in heaven and Earth.

Mabel Jam

Chapter 5

Creative Visualizations to Achieve Erotic Magic

Creative visualization is the technique that the mind uses to convert desires into reality. With creative visualization, we utilize the imagination to create an image, idea, or situation that we desire. Thinking of a trip, a work project, or something we want to buy carries us almost instantly to a series of images. The psychic force and consistency that we employ in creating these visualizations is what will provide the energy needed to achieve them.

Through visualization, we are able to develop the power of creation and make conscious choices about what kind of life we desire to live.

Our thought process is creative. It creates our surroundings, especially everything on which we focus, and what we understand. Sometimes this is conscious, but most of the time it is subconscious. If we want to change our world and our relationships, we don't have to change much; we just have to start by changing our thinking.

There are seven principles for effective, creative visualizations that achieve positive results:

1. Thought has the power to transform.

2. One is and possesses that which one thinks or believes.

3. We have many thoughts every second. We should think consciously.

4. We can change everything that we think.

5. We should always be alert to what we desire and think.

6. We should control our thoughts rather than permitting our thoughts to control us.

7. We should exercise our thinking daily. Time and space are necessary for focusing energy to transform, learn, and evolve.

There are only two steps involved in creating an excellent creative visualization:

Complete respiration

Mental concentration

Before beginning the visualization exercise, clearly define what it is that you wish to achieve. It is very important to specify a time limit or a finite objective in every affirmation that you desire to convert into reality. For example, you may wish to improve communication with your partner during dinner or during a magical erotic act, or you may desire not to have any problems with your relationship today.

We'll use the first example. Visualize yourself with your partner having dinner at home. Don't try to imagine the situation as if it were a movie playing in your mind; rather, try to feel with all of your senses that what you are visualizing is real. Later, imagine a scene where there is little communication between you and discard this image from your thoughts. Add to this imaginary action the word CANCELLED. After getting rid of all negative possibilities, imagine a cordial and affectionate dinner featuring comfortable conversation. Visualize this for a few minutes; no more than three, with all of the details that you wish would come true. Limit yourself to two creative visualizations per day until your desires manifest in reality. Once you have achieved both visualizations, continue working with new ones, but never do more than two images per day.

If we have the capacity to dream, we also have the power to make our dreams become reality. The mind is very literal and organized and we can direct it as we choose. To discover pleasure beyond what we know, we can utilize the infinite energy of our body through the seven chakras. To correctly stimulate each one of these, learn how to awaken them, visualizing their corresponding colors. Once it is understood, the visualization process can create its own methods for realizing its wishes. By experimenting with a more extraordinary and fuller life, we will advance in our quest to achieve magical meditation.

Magical Meditation with a Partner

Meditation is a natural state of our being. To achieve it, one must recognize the foundation of all of our experiences and by doing so arrive at a higher level of consciousness. Meditating awakens the fundamental and innate intelligence of being, the spiritual light, and is fundamental to everything that we perceive. It helps us become conscious of the possibility of living awakened and free spiritually.

Meditation distances individuals from the countless activities of the body and mind, and directs them to a clearer understanding of themselves. It's not that those everyday activities or experiences are contradictory or incompatible with being spiritually awakened, but rather, meditation separates us from these things so as to simplify finding ourselves internally.

A confused mind that is trapped in ideas, experiences, desires, and impulses only engenders conflict. When the mind is clear, precise, and capable of profound reasoning, it more easily discovers a meditative state, and can clearly recognize the true feeling of love.

Through meditation, we experience a way of living that recognizes reality for the way it truly is, without losing ourselves in conceptual illusions or emotional attachments that are nothing more than pieces of that unfathomable and immense reality. Every human act and practice should be meditative—in other words, enlightened, awake, and free from deceit.

Be a little more free each day by recognizing your feelings for what they are, and letting your innate intelligence guide your every act—not the ideas the accumulate in your memory or the judgments you've made.

To meditate, live with sincerity. Look at yourself naked in the mirror. Embrace the reality of the universe that encircles you, because it is your home.

Meditation is Delighting in Your Own Being

Meditation will help you develop sensitivity and a wonderful feeling of belonging to this world. Your level of sensitivity will increase to the point that even the smallest blade of grass acquires immense importance. Sensitivity allows us to understand that the blade of grass is as important to existence as the stars; without it, existence would be diminished. Conscious meditation, with a partner or alone, gives us:

Increased longevity

Harmony of the body, mind, and spirit

Maintained youthful appearance

Increased sexual energy

Balanced glandular excretion

Recovered emotional harmony

Balanced energy centers

Stress elimination

Increased ability to concentrate

Expanded creativity and memory

Increased willingness and determination

Lowered heart rate (number of times the heart beats per minute)

Diminished level of cholesterol in the blood

Less muscular tension

The ability to be awake and alert in any circumstance

States of Consciousness and Meditation

Conscious meditation facilitates the elevation of your consciousness level. There are three levels:

1. Human consciousness. This is related to daily acts and mundane things, the normal communication where we don't seek a specific goal, but rather, we express our need to communicate.

2. The consciousness of lovers. This is the plane where two beings long to unite. Love elevates them toward a superior human state.

3. Divine consciousness. The mind is part of the totality of the universe. This level achieves oneness with the infinite through silence, or through the verbal or mental repetition of mantras utilized to mobilize each chakra.

Exercise: Achieve Divine Consciousness

In a state of relaxation, in the nude, and in front of your partner, begin to visualize the triple flame of the three colors of your heart. By doing this, a spiritual light will radiate like a torch toward the heart of your partner. Your partner in magic should do the exercise at the same time.

Next, visualize your partner wrapped in those three colors. If you can't imagine it, before doing the ritual, observe a candle's flame and you will see the three colors and the light they provide.

Now, imagine that fire or heat comes from your heart and is received by your partner. This exercise is high in spiritual intensity and provokes a stronger and more complete union before sexual contact.

Meditation with a Partner to Develop Consciousness

The partners should be lying down and relaxed. With the eyes closed, relax your mind, concentrating on deep breathing. Observe the path that air travels when it leaves and enters the body. Now, practice a breathing harmonization technique. Inhale at the same time, hold in the breath, exhale, and pause before beginning again together. Perform at least three complete breaths: inhale, maintain, exhale, maintain.

Observe what passes through your mind, your thoughts, like the rhythm of your body and your emotions. If memories appear, do not repress them. Only observe them and let them go. Imagine your mind like a sky filled with clouds. Observe the colors of the clouds and their density. Every cloud represents a thought or a feeling. Now, free every cloud until the sky is completely clear, blue, and illuminated. Observe the mind until it becomes empty and tranquil.

Do this exercise every day for ten minutes. In every session, you will achieve a higher state of consciousness.

Meditation with Magical Mandalas

The magical circles known as mandalas are symbols that can be used to access the magic of eroticism. According to Tantric philosophy, there was a time when the gods found a nameless energy that vibrated perfectly between the sky and the Earth. They called it *mandala*, which in Hindi means *circle* or *circuit*.

The mandala works like a battery in the electromagnetic field of our body and mind, concentrating all images or symbols of different dimensions and cultures. Because of the high level of chemical-cellular transformation that is produced by sexual activity, the cerebral circuits are accelerated in such a way as to, sometimes, not allow one to achieve an optimal sexual relationship. This chemistry can be unblocked through meditation with mandalas.

Mandalas have a psychic function and are wrapped in an energy flow that follows a certain parameter for its utilization during visualization. The correct way to meditate is by concentrating on a point in the center of the mandala until the image is integrated in your mind. Later, let your attention expand outward from the center.

Meditation with the different mandalas will unblock the energy that impedes the formation of a full sexual relationship. Every mandala is attuned to a singular harmony, like a love song. If you want to create your own mandala for meditation, you can make one with a partner or by yourself, utilizing it together or individually.

The circular shape of the mandala functions as an integrating element because in the circle, all geometric shapes unite. When constructing a mandala, it is possible to include inside of the integrating circle other figures, such as:

The circle represents the oneness of all being and the origin of the Divine.

The triangle is related to the divine light of creation.

The square represents matter and our inner selves made manifest.

When creating a mandala, it is important to express the polarities—feminine and masculine—as in every connection of living relationships. One of the most popular magic circles in the world is the Taoist mandala of ying and yang, which symbolizes the balance between the feminine and masculine in the Universe. The dark part, the ying, corresponds to the feminine and the light part, the yang, to the masculine. The Taoists used it as a symbol of the perfect path.

It is possible to create your own, unique mandala; you can even make a different one every day. You can do it on your own or with your partner to enhance sexual magic. The correspondences of the colors that compose the circle, or each geometric figure inside the mandala, are:

Black: Color that absorbs light. It is associated with feminine energy, with the dark side of the Tao mandala, but its effect can be different according to how it is utilized.

Blue: A cool color that helps to level out high anxiety and to control attacks of obsessive sexual attraction.

Brown: Is associated with constancy and friendship with those people that help us grow spiritually. Brown can be utilized to fix a very conflicted sexual relationship. Also used to attract money and friendship.

Green: Associated with nature and living energy. Its vibrations are hypnotic and create total calm in every living system of an organism, acting directly on the psyche.

Gray: Neutral color *par excellence*. This can be used to neutralize external forces and to create a favorable environment to understand more clearly what is happening to us.

Orange: Has sedative effects and directly impacts the central nervous system. Orange increases the capacity to concentrate awareness. For that reason, it is important to always use this color in the center of an energetic mandala.

Pink: Preserves love in sexual relations, in both stable and unstable relationships. Pink integrates love and erotic passion into one connection.

Red: Symbolizes sexual power, increases eroticism, provides power and resistance, fills the blood with oxygen, and cleans toxins.

Sky-blue: A great spiritual generator. Magnetizes people's surroundings, attracting glorious states of peace, protection, and security.

Violet: The color of transformation of negative emotions. It acts as a multiprocessor of negative thoughts because it corresponds to the spiritual manifesto.

White: Used in purification rituals because it is related to cleanliness that comes before sexual relations or a romantic union. White breaks with adverse conditions and increases spiritual faith.

Yellow: The natural stimulant of the emotions. Yellow functions perfectly for harmonizing and manifesting personal desires and ambitions.

Meditation with mandalas, conscious meditation with a partner, and every exercise that you do will transform your days into a life surprisingly full of love, magic, wisdom, and power.

I desire to draw a map of the route to your being,
and travel through each door of your soul to give
you pleasure. While I embark upon the abundant
sea of your body, we slide until we reach
our final destination
the only refuge where the eternal flame resides.

Mabel Jam

Chapter 6

The Magical Positions
of the Kama Sutra

Each couple has a sexual position that is used more often, but we recommend looking for variation and novelty to keep the interest alive in your relationship. We believe that the main reason that couples separate and the main reason for infidelity is the lack of varied pleasure and the monotony of life as a couple.

We emphasize here the Kama Sutra, an ancient Sanskrit text on the subject of love and sexual technique, as well as Taoist books that describe in detail the diverse postures. If we wish to have a relationship filled with creativity we must know all the positions that we could use during the sex act with our partner.

Kama means consciousness of pleasure by means of the five senses, the mind and the soul. *Sutra* means teaching. By following the Kama Sutra you can experience pleasure with the five senses of your soul. According to the Kama Sutra, harmony is achieved when a man and a woman live like one body and one soul. The study of the laws of Kama Sutra is said to transport the human being to plenitude and harmony, to reach real happiness.

Andromaco's Posture

The man lies on his back while his partner kneels or squats over him with her breasts raised. The woman controls the depth and the rhythm of the penetration and she can set free her fantasies to control her partner.

The advantage of this position for the woman is that she has total control.

The man has his hands free to caress his partner's breasts, thighs or clitoris. This position allows good stimulation of the G-spot.

Andromaco's posture

Lovers' Union

Both lovers stand facing each other. The man rubs his penis against his lover's vulva. After a few moments of stimulation, the vulva will open naturally to allow a shallow penetration.

This posture is very practical and can be improvised at any time. It allows a good stimulation of the clitoris and the glans.

Lovers' union

Face to Face

This is the most classic and universal position used by both beginners and experts. As the couple lies down, the man places his body between the woman's legs to penetrate her. A variation calls for placing a pillow below the woman's buttocks to modify the angle of the vagina and allow for a better and deeper penetration.

This is a comfortable and natural posture for both partners. The man enjoys freedom of movement, and during intercourse the couple can look at each other and kiss.

Face to face

The Tiger

Starting from the face to face position, the woman raises her legs to her torso. Changing the angle of her legs allows her to feel a variety of sensations. She can also rest her feet on her partner's buttocks to increase the pressure on the pelvis.

When the woman lifts her legs, the penetration becomes deeper and it is easier to control the sensations. The man's pelvic bone rubs against the vulva directly stimulating the clitoris.

The tiger

The Courtesan

The man kneels down to penetrate his partner who is sitting on the edge of the bed or a chair. She can wrap her legs around her partner's waist. There is a variant in which the woman leans against a table or desk while her lover, who is standing up, penetrates her.

This is a comfortable position for both partners, and allows an excellent penetration with a wide range of pelvic movements.

The courtesan

The Cow (or the Dog)

This is a classic posture favored all over the world for the intense sensations it produces. The woman kneels and places her hands on the floor as she is penetrated by her partner, who is also kneeling. The woman can place some pillows underneath her knees if desired.

This position produces excellent stimulation of the front wall of the vagina and the G-spot. Penetration is vigorous and deep. The man's hands are free to stimulate his partner's clitoris and breasts. This posture encourages the man's fantasies of domination and sexual control.

The cow (or the dog)

Perfect Alignment

The woman lies atop the man with her legs open for easy penetration. Once the penis is inside, she closes her legs so that both bodies are perfectly aligned. Then the woman initiates stimulation by rubbing her body against her partner's body.

This is a very intimate position and it offers increased contact between partners. The vaginal walls are more compressed and allow for deeper sensations.

Perfect alignment

The Elephant

Starting from the cow's or dog's posture, the woman lies face-down so that the man can cover her completely. She can leave her legs open to ease penetration or contract her buttocks to hold the penis firmly inside the vagina. A variation allows the man to rest on his forearms to take his weight off his partner a bit and penetrate her more deeply.

This position generates an excellent stimulation of the front wall of the vagina and the G-spot, and the man can place his hand beneath the woman to stimulate the clitoris. This posture produces the most contact between partners.

The elephant

The Horseman

The man lies on his back while his partner kneels over him, wrapping her legs around his legs. The woman controls the direction and force of the movements to increase the sensations on the clitoris and the vaginal walls or to urge the man to achieve orgasm quickly.

The woman is more free and active in this position; she can choose the rhythm, speed and type of movement. The man adopts a passive attitude, which allows him to concentrate on the pleasurable sensations, and at the same time he can caress his partner.

The horseman

Indra

The man kneels. The woman lies on her back, with her legs against her partner's torso. The man leans forward to compress the woman's thighs against her chest.

This posture allows for maximum penetration, while the compression of the stomach and vagina produce a strong stimulation.

Indra

The Octopus

The woman lies on her back resting her buttocks on her partner's knees and legs. The man can lift her slightly to change the angle and the depth of the penetration.

This is a deep and comfortable posture for both partners, and both have their hands free.

The octopus

The Tortoise

Starting with the perfect alignment position, the man opens his legs so that his partner's thighs go in between them.

This is a very intimate posture that allows more contact between partners. The sensations are very strong since the vagina is compressed against the penis.

The tortoise

The Plow

Lying on her back, with her buttocks at the edge of the bed, the woman wraps her legs around the man's waist. The man kneels on the floor to penetrate her, keeping his penis horizontal, level with her vagina. A variation has the man standing up and the woman lying on a desk or table.

The horizontal alignment of the penis and the vagina produces unique sensations, which are different from the sensations felt in more common positions. This is a deep penetration that stimulates the vaginal walls well.

The plow

The Anvil

The woman lies on her back as she places her feet on her partner's shoulders. This posture allows for a very deep penetration. It is not recommended at the beginning of foreplay, since the vagina has not yet reached its maximum size and it may not have enough lubrication.

When done correctly, the woman can have strong sensations, especially if the man ejaculates in this posture.

The anvil

The Eagle

The partners lie on their sides and wrap their arms and legs around each other. The woman surrounds the waist of her partner with her legs. The man folds his legs slightly to ease penetration.

This is a very intimate posture that offers maximum contact between the lovers. There is a good penetration if the man folds his thighs against the thighs of his partner.

The eagle

The Missionary's Dance

Starting with the face-to-face position, the woman tightens her buttocks and arches her trunk upwards, undulating her waist in a circular-lateral-vertical movement.

This position produces good stimulation, and a fast orgasm for the man.

The missionary's dance

The Pillar

Both partners kneel on the bed facing each other. The woman places her legs on her partner's thighs, guiding his penis to her vagina.

This intimate posture, recommended in the Tantra, allows the lovers to caress and hold each other.

The pillar

The Magpie's Fusion

This is a variation of the goddess's posture (see below) in which the man sits on a chair instead of a bed. It is a comfortable position since it is more stable and the movements are easier. It can be used as the beginning of a sequence starting with the suspended union and the pillar and finishing with the fac-to-face posture.

This position allows for a deep penetration and a wide range of vertical movements.

The magpie's fusion

The Antelope

Kneeling on the floor, the woman lifts her body holding to the edge of the bed. The man kneels to penetrate her from behind. In a variant of this posture, the woman can keep her legs open at each side of her partner's legs to widen the vaginal opening. She can also close her thighs to compress the vagina around the penis.

This position is perfect to stimulate the front walls of the vagina and the G-spot. At the same time, the man can stimulate his partner's clitoris and breasts.

The antelope

The Goddess

The man sits on the bed with his back against the wall or headboard for better support. The woman sits atop him, guiding his penis toward her vagina, while she wraps her legs around his waist. The woman makes circular movements to stimulate her clitoris and vaginal walls.

This is also considered a very intimate posture. Both partners may kiss each other and the man can lick her breasts. The deep penetration is accompanied by a good stimulation of the clitoris. This is an excellent posture to delay orgasm when a man suffers from early ejaculation.

The goddess

The Oyster

The woman lies on her back with her thighs bent toward her torso. The man holds her from the knees using her thighs as a support to allow the rhythmic movement.

This position permits a deep penetration and a wide range of movements. The vagina is compressed against the penis, so both partners receive an excellent stimulation.

The oyster

The Boa

The woman lies on her back, slightly on her side, placing her legs on her partner's hips. The man moves his penis to penetrate her gently. She will have to tighten her thighs to hold the penis in place and achieve better sensations.

This is a posture for making love at ease and without any hurry.

The boa

The Ying and the Yang

The man sits in a squatting position on a solid and stable surface. The woman sits on his knees, facing him. For more stability, he can rest his back against a wall or any other vertical support.

This is a fun and original posture.

The ying and the yang

The Star

The woman lies on her back with her legs apart. The man places one leg between her legs and penetrates her from the side, leaning on his arm on the opposite side. Stimulation increases as he rubs his thigh against the clitoris.

This posture is interesting since the penetration is done from the side and it produces different sensations both for the man and the woman. The man's thighs rub the vulva and the clitoris. Both have one hand free to caress or embrace each other.

The star

Kisses, Foreplay, and Pleasure

As we mentioned before, erotic kisses are a fundamental part of sexual contact for a couple. They show love and desire, and at the same time fortify the bond between the couple. That is why learning how to kiss and to take advantage of erotic kisses is a very pleasant practice. It is an objective unto itself, with marvelous and unsuspected consequences.

The act of kissing is not as complex as the sexual act itself and requires less from the couple, even though it may be as or more gratifying than sex. Kissing does not offer problems such as premature ejaculation, impotency, lack of lubrication, inhibited desires or cultural and psychological repressions that affect the pleasure of the sexual union. Even though our Western culture sees kissing as a mere demonstration of love, the power of a kiss is greater than one might think. The magic of love recognizes this and explores it as a genuine and significant way of achieving gratification.

We can all distinguish the difference between simple, chaste lip contact and a deep and passionate kiss. Some women—especially those practicing Tao—can only achieve an orgasm with a true kiss. For Taoists these erotic kisses are like a divine revelation. They encourage kissing due to its low risk and high pleasure.

To experience a passionate, erotic kiss we need to know how to use our lips, our tongue, and mouth to make the most of this intimate moment. The mouth is equivalent to the jade hammer—the penis—and to the jade door—the vulva—as the skin and membranes are very sensitive. The mouth, lips, and tongue are organs that have voluntary movement, as opposed to the genital organs that have involuntary movement that we cannot always control.

Intercourse requires a great physical effort whereas erotic kisses do not. No matter how tired the couple may be, it is possible to have a long kissing session full of eroticism—intimate, tender, communicative, magical, and marvelous.

Kissing and hugging have a fundamental role during the sexual act and they are considered the signs of a more intimate bond between the couple. One may kiss the lower lips, the eyes, the cheeks, the head, the mouth, the breasts, the shoulders, the armpits, the navel, and the erotic zones of one's lover. The following list of kisses has been extracted from Taoist books about the art of love.

The *Ghatika* kiss. The woman kisses with passion, covering the eyes of the man. She closes her eyes and introduces her tongue into his mouth and moves it from one side to the other.

Hanuvatra. It starts with inciting and playful lip movements. The kiss is given later.

Pindita, or sugar kiss. The woman takes the lips of her partner with her fingers, licks them with her tongue and bites them a bit.

Platibodha, or wake up kiss. The man who has been absent returns and finds his partner asleep. He kisses her, gradually becoming more forceful until she wakes up.

The reconciliation kiss. The man keeps his lips against the lips of his partner until she is no longer angry.

Samaushtha. The woman takes the lips of her partner with her lips, holding them and dancing around them with her tongue.

Samputa or coffer kiss. The lovers kiss the inside of their mouths.

Sphurita. The woman brings her mouth near her partner's mouth, as he kisses the lower lip and plays as if rejecting it.

Tiryak, or oblique kiss. The man stands behind or beside his partner, placing his hand on her chin. He lifts her chin as she looks up, and then he kisses her lip, placing it in between his teeth and biting it gently.

Uttaroshta, or upper lip kiss. The woman takes the man's lower lip while he holds her upper lip between his teeth as they bite each other.

Like magic, kissing is an old art. Practice it every day.

What do we feel when we kiss and hold each other? Excitement, self-esteem, security, approval, contentment, strength, devotion, spirituality, protection, enthusiasm, happiness. Kissing relates psychologically to the most primitive contact between human beings, and it reminds us, in a conscious way, of our needs like food, pleasure, appetite, desire, rejection—all we associate with survival.

Make a list of all the people you would like to kiss or hug and explain why. Think why you do not demonstrate your affection more often. If one of those people is your partner, wake him or her with a kiss. If you do not live together, call your partner over the phone and send him or her a kiss. Send your partner a message every day that includes a kiss and a hug. Do the same with all the other people on the list. According to your relationship with that person and your comfort level, choose between a kiss or a hug as you consider appropriate.

Love Rituals

Perform a love ritual every time you feel depressed, when you have problems with your partner, if you feel low self-esteem, if you feel you are not desired or loved, or in any similar situations. Relax and find a quiet place. You may use aromas for the environment such as incense or perfumes. Listen to some calming music and dress in comfortable clothes. Lie down on a comfortable surface where you feel at ease.

Visualize each of the cells of your body, and imagine that they transform into small kisses with different characteristics and colors: red, pink, violet; sweet, healthy, passionate, sensual, and attractive.

Imagine that you hug your body and caress it in your mind, or wrap your arms around your body. When you really feel that you love yourself, imagine the person you desire is in front of you.

Hug and embrace that person in your imagination. You will see how the energy of love can make miracles happen in your relationship. Now visualize that the kisses and hugs come in your direction.

In this chapter we have explored the ancient art of kissing and love-making; next we will analyze problems between the partners and find the solutions.

A man and a woman . . .
Man is the flying eagle.
Woman, the singing nightingale.
To fly is to conquer space.
To sing is to conquer the soul.
Man is the temple.
Woman is the shrine.
Before the temple we discover ourselves,
before the shrine we kneel...
In short, Man is found where Earth finishes,
A woman, where Heaven begins.

Victor Hugo

Chapter 7

Solve Your Problems as a Couple Through the Magic of Sex

The vital life force is governed by the most primary instincts of the human being and is directly related to the sexual needs of the individual. However, sexual repression in all its forms impedes that life force.

Many persons repress and ignore these emotions due to social and cultural conditionings; this creates a false sense of guilt and the impossibility of getting to know oneself. When a person represses himself or herself in this way, the vital energy is blocked and this blockage diminishes the creative force and the unifying power of life, affecting the physical and psychological health of that person.

The fear and guilt associated with these emotions can be overcome. Once a person accepts that no emotion is able to be completely controlled by the conscious mind, that person may bring light to those hidden feelings that lie abandoned in the deeper part of his or her mind. We must not fear those irrational emotions; we must be aware of them and simply let them be free in our thoughts without judging or repressing them.

How to Avoid Sexual Impotency

As children, we explore our bodies with curiosity. During our teenage years we show interest in sexual topics, eventually developing certain fantasies and achieving our first sexual relationship.

In spite of sex being a natural part of life, both men and women experience social taboos surrounding sex that prevent a satisfying and conscious sexuality. Most of us have inherited a heavy burden associated with sexuality based on social conditioning.

Most people cannot talk about their own sexuality without feeling embarrassed. Few can mention their genitals in a loud voice without blushing. Some cannot even touch their own bodies in an intimate moment, or look at someone's nakedness without feeling guilty, nervous, or bothered.

Intimacy and foreplay must be accepted by both partners so that they can express themselves freely through their bodies and emotions. When one of the partners rejects himself or herself—be it his or her emotions or body—that person cannot accept intimacy. Fear, anguish, or anxiety towards a couple's intimate contact causes a critical barrier to healthy sexuality. That barrier or disconnect brings about sexual or emotional impotency.

Our body has an incredible ability to sense different levels of pleasure, but it can also block those sensors for a variety of reasons. An example of blockage is early male ejaculation as a form of impotence—in other words, ejaculation with a minimum of sexual stimulation or immediately after penetration. This lack of ability to hold an erection prevents the woman from achieving a satisfactory orgasm, and also produces frustration on the emotional level. When a woman feels blocked or inhibited because she does not understand her body or her emotions, she can produce impotence in the relationship. As the couple experiences a negative situation over and over again, they feel frustrated and may begin to feel apprehensive about sexual encounters.

Sexual magic includes techniques to avoid these blockages and increase pleasure for the couple.

Orgasm Physiology

At orgasm, the man feels pleasurable contractions that culminate in ejaculation. His excitement is localized in his genitals. Afterward, his sexual intensity decreases. For a woman, on the other hand, the process is totally different. Normally, she feels pleasurable contractions that spread throughout her pelvis. But, unlike the man, that is just the beginning of sex for her.

The woman does not experience flaccid genital organs, like a man, so she is able to experience multiple orgasms. The sensation is intensified as she has one orgasm after another, whereas the man needs some recovery time between erections.

How Can an Erection be Maintained?

During sexual stimulation, the man's genital nerves relax the valves of the spongy tissue of the penis, allowing increased blood flow and enlarging the organ.

The erection can be produced by physiological factors, not necessarily erotic stimulation. That is the classic case of the "morning erection" due to a full bladder. However, most erections are produced by brain stimulation and, for that reason, they are governed by the psyche. Most cases of sexual impotence are related to psychological rather than physiological problems. Therefore it is possible for a man to overcome impotence.

Erotic magic teaches us that knowing how our body works is the key to controlling it. In this case, it is possible to stimulate and exercise the muscles that control the penis to facilitate an erection. The man must start by concentrating on his genital organ and sensing the area that originates the force that engorges it; that is, the area below the testicles. The man may self-stimulate that area with massage to feel how the flow of blood increases and begins to erect the penis. This exercise plus controlled breathing will allow an erection and help to maintain it during intercourse.

How to Control Ejaculation

Tantric Buddhism, like sexual magic, has developed techniques to control ejaculation. This exercise requires the control of the urinary and genital organs, especially the sphincters. A good start is to begin controlling urination during brief periods. When you feel the need to urinate, you can release a tiny amount and then keep the rest inside for a few seconds. This process is repeated till the bladder is empty. During retention, the man must contract his sexual organ and this will help contract the muscle that produces erections.

How to Control Oneself When we Reach the Limit of our Desire

When the man is close to ejaculation, he must pause and contract the muscles of the penis again. At the beginning, it may be helpful to withdraw from his partner's body for a few moments.

How to Recover Desire in a Relationship

Through sexual magic, it is possible to recover the lost fire in a relationship. Many couples maintain a healthy sexual relationship because of their love for and happiness with each other. Other couples keep the relationship exciting due to a strong physical attraction. But as time passes, many factors such as everyday life, unfortunate comments, routine, fatigue, lack of communication, and economic and personal problems introduce negativity and erode interest in sexual relationships. These are some of the difficulties that we have to avoid.

Never Tell a Man:

"Look at the hair on the pillow. My love, you are losing your hair." Never say something like that when you are initiating or concluding a sexual encounter. A man may react in a negative way and try to find another woman to reaffirm his own self-esteem.

"What is going on? It is not working today?" This may be the worst of all comments—never make any negative remarks about his sexual organ. He might answer, "Exactly, you irritate me so much that I cannot get excited."

Never Tell a Woman:

"You are getting fat, have you noticed it?" No woman likes to hear that she is becoming less attractive or needs to start a diet.

"I like that actress; she is so beautiful." A woman may feel she is incapable of reaching the level of beauty that you are admiring.

"Ah, it is delicious, but when my ex-wife cooked . . ." The ghosts from previous relationships can bother any woman, and even more so when the two women are compared.

If you want to get rid of your partner, remember these phrases. Otherwise, if you want to keep the relationship, forget them forever.

Strategies to Rekindle Passion

Introduce some mystery in your relationship to build an enigmatic atmosphere. Keep some innocent secrets to attract her or his interest.

Be patient and learn to wait. Sometimes, due to external situations, our partner may not respond to our emotional or sexual needs.

Add a little bit of boldness at the right time to achieve excellent results. Try it!

Use your intuition. After a less-than-satisfying moment with your partner, try to find an ideal moment to rekindle passion. Bring to your mind images of happy times. Take the first step and follow your intuition.

Try an erotic ritual every day (see chapter 1).

Be supportive and understanding. Your partner may feel some insecurity, but take care not to take advantage of him or her. Try to fortify his or her self-esteem.

Make an effort to come up with pleasant surprises. Presents may make her happy and can stimulate the relationship, especially if they are reminders of the best times of the couple.

Use romanticism and seduction, incorporating your special talents, desires and abilities.

Be original. Find your true inner self and communicate from it with your partner.

Cultivate a winning attitude. Happiness is a choice we can make at any time and at any place. Your thoughts and beliefs create your emotions, whether positive or negative. It is your choice.

Set Your Fantasies Free

The couple becomes more free when both partners can liberate their fantasies. Study dreams to try to discover the reasons for any blockages that may be affecting your sexual relationship. If you have never analyzed the content of your dreams, this is a good time to start, alone or with your partner, as you prefer. This is an opportunity to learn how your sexual desires work and to learn about the desires of your partner.

Sexual instinct, when expressed freely, creates a bond and sets you free from negative thoughts or emotions. In order to achieve a magical relationship based on stability, love and mutual respect, it is vital to understand the deepest instincts that each human being has.

Almost everyone has fantasies about situations that are not accepted by society, and nearly everyone wonders if they should be ashamed of such thoughts for moral reasons. The problem is not only the limited scope of what is considered "acceptable," but that we allow shame to control us. Is OK for a woman to imagine that she is seducing a man and feel happy and at ease? Is OK for a man to submit to a very strong woman? Is it OK to discuss fantasies with a friend of the same sex?

Fantasies are a game within our minds, the highest level of mental activity, but why can't we accept them? Basically, fear. Fear of being exposed and considered sick, perverted, or sexual. As we try repeatedly to avoid fantasies, we tend to block our relationships with other people, but feelings of judgment and rejection of these thoughts won't stop them.

As we feel more at ease with ourselves, we begin to recognize our self worth. We feel we deserve to be loved and we are ready to accept our sexual fantasies. The acceptance of our sexual fantasies, whether light or dark, can be fostered through understanding. When we understand what we call the erotic marks of our psyche—images, feelings, and sensations that stimulate us sexually—we can reduce what is blocking our fantasies.

Exercise: Unblock Your Fantasies

Find a comfortable position and close your eyes. You may listen to some music to help you relax.

First step: Take a deep breath and let your body relax each time you exhale. Think about the sexual, erotic or romantic fantasies you have. They may be fantasies used during masturbation, while you make love, or when you walk in the sun. Pay attention to your physical reactions.

Second step: Remember and compile fantasies from your childhood, adolescence, or adult life. Imagine telling your fantasies to a group of people. Who are they? How do they react? What do they think?

Third step: Imagine now that you are telling your fantasies to your partner, his or her parents, to a priest, or to your boss. Have fantasies about people who are in a position of authority, or about people you admire or like. Pay attention on how you feel on each occasion, how your body responds, what type of judgments you may offer.

Fourth step: When you are done, open your eyes slowly and take a sheet of paper. Write down a description of each fantasy and the emotional or physical response that it brings. Do not censor yourself as you write. If you feel ashamed, write about that feeling.

Show compassion and acceptance toward yourself. Remember to breathe, to listen to your own feelings, and to be ready to explain what you feel at each moment as you write. The experiences you explore in this exercise create the ideal conditions to understand yourself better.

If you do this exercise with your partner, you can free your relationship from the ghost of shame, and you will be able to eliminate the negative beliefs that block your eroticism.

Remember that you cannot control the world, but you can control your thoughts. It is very important to take care of your body, and to do so you must understand your emotions. Try to practice these exercises with your partner; this way you will both liberate yourselves from stress and will generate the secretion of endorphins that replenish your chemistry of passion and vitality.

We, as human beings, can find pleasure in eroticism and in spiritual fusion with our partner, as well as in the physical well being produced by the miraculous art of love making.

Each of us is responsible for what happens to us
and we have the power to decide what we want to be.
You are today the result of your decisions and actions
from the past. Tomorrow, you will be the result of
what you did today.

Vivekananda

Chapter 8

Sacred Plan for
the Eternal Partners

As Vivekananda affirms in the beginning of this chapter, we are all responsible for what happens to us because our divinity resides within us. Don't wait for the ideal moment to be happy. Believe, love, work, carry out a magical act every day, and create your happiness.

In order to have harmonious relationships and wonderful opportunities, one should understand how feelings work. As we explained in chapter 4, the emotional body is that in which all of the emotions are concentrated. How can we control them in our favor? The first step is to clarify how we speak of our emotions.

In our daily language, we express our emotions on a positive-negative scale. For example, one may ask, "Do you feel well?" to which another may reply, "No, I don't feel well." We also indicate the intensity or level of our emotions, for instance, "I feel really well," or "I felt very bad." In order to describe the intensity of each emotion, we use words like little or very, according to the intensity of each emotion. This is how we compose the description of an emotion. We say "I feel really supported" (positive) or "I feel very disappointed" (negative).

Every situation provokes emotions, and emotions can affect the physical body. When they do, they are referred to as "psychosomatic disorders." The most common are those that affect the skin and the respiratory, gastrointestinal, reproductive, and cardio-circulatory systems. Asthma, frigidity, sexual impotency, tachycardia (abnormally rapid heartbeat), fainting, and so on, are conditions that may be tied to psycho-emotional aspects.

Part of magical wisdom is exploring the emotions; this will help us learn not to exhaust our emotions by releasing them into our body or our personal relationships. The world of emotions has always been considered conflictive, especially when a person perceives an internal discord between the emotional and the rational. Here are some tips for learning to control one's emotions:

Maintain a tranquil attitude in response to stimuli that provoke fear or anger.

Control your language. Control over words helps discipline the emotions.

Learn to read subliminal messages from people who want to influence your emotional state.

Clear your mind of thoughts every day.

Learn to project your thoughts toward new situations, comparing them with other experiences.

Evaluate the emotions that are provoked in others.

Control your breathing. When facing a strong emotional situation, breathe slowly.

Divine Tenderness is Magic

Once we understand how to control our emotions, we can free them from negative associations. By doing this, we can experience positive feelings everyday in order to fully share them with others.

Can you remember the last time you waited for someone with open arms to lavish them with loving words and expressions of tenderness? Get a notebook or journal to write down some ideas for nurturing your partner.

Think over what has happened in the past few weeks. How many times did the person you love take you in their arms by surprise? How many times did you feel an absence of affection in your relationship? Do you feel that you have lost forever the glorious passion that you had in the first days you spent with your partner? Can you reproduce that passing, passionate love with the same enthusiasm? How long can someone suffer from desire before asking for the contact and affection that they lack in their daily life?

The first step toward change is to stop complaining. If you wish to have a more pleasant connection with your partner, it is important to avoid bad intentions and exhausting moments of discussion. It is indispensable to have at your disposal some tools that will improve each encounter:

1. Laughter. Laughing at oneself and finding something positive about awkward situations can provoke feelings of tenderness.

2. Silence. Learn to notice and value a companionable silence. Those silences are instant tender moments.

3. Surprise. Routine is the worst enemy of affection. A couple can only transform this state of inertia when they learn to think about those small but important details that cause happiness in the other. Discovering how to nurture a feeling of tenderness every day is an incredible game with thousands of creative combinations. Write on your calendar (or in your notebook) a list of surprises for your loved one.

4. Be timely. The most difficult point in a loving relationship is recognizing the right moments to bring up topics that bother or irritate us and block the pleasure of the relationship.

5. Be generous. It is important to give without the expectation of receiving anything in return.

6. Sensitivity. Be alert to that which your partner desires to express. Words don't always accurately describe feelings. Many times, profound emotions are found hiding behind words.

To be able to love and relax, dedicating oneself with body and mind to one's lover is neither a dream nor an antiquated illusion. Permitting your partner and yourself to enjoy some true tenderness, even if only for a few moments, is a nice break from daily life.

To maintain passion, a couple not only needs affection, they also need attention. One should devote one's care, love, and dedication to a sexual relationship just as one would to a profession, course of study, or family. Sexuality can be a paradise on Earth if the partners desire to surpass mediocrity and their routine, looking for love as the only purpose here and now.

Imagine what it would be like to make love if there were no performance anxiety or disproportionate concern for the experience of your partner. All of the techniques recommended in this book are subordinate to this basic principle: there is nothing more essential than being compassionate and affectionate with yourself and with your partner. Since we live in a society centered on doing, we should permit ourselves a large margin of error while we learn simply to be.

Sexual Rhythm, Step by Step

Men and women possess distinct sexual response times. If you hope to get the most from your magical exploration, you should be aware of these natural rhythms.

1. The first stage is sexual impulse, which is directly related to mutual attraction. This rhythmic level is marked by the interest that each individual sparks in his or her companion.

2. The second is arousal, which generally manifests more slowly in women and more quickly in men. Arousal stems from the erotic attraction that is discovered in the first rhythm and grows and deepens as we stimulate the erogenous zones of our lover.

3. The third, the orgasm, is the result of the previous stages. As with dance, achieving orgasm is an emotional response that is instinctive to a large degree.

4. The fourth rhythm, the consummation, is the effect of maximum pleasure. In this level, an outpouring of spiritual energy crosses the limits of physical satisfaction and awakens profound feelings in the lovers. It is only possible to arrive at this level of ecstasy by mutually giving ourselves to the other and following the loving rhythm. When both lovers adapt their sexual response to their partner, the sexual act does not conclude with the orgasm. On the contrary, after the physical conclusion of sexual pleasure, both partners are replenished with an influx of emotional and spiritual energy.

Exercise: The Mirror Game

When the two participants in the erotic relationship have difficulty finding a mutually satisfying rhythm, they can do the mirror game exercise, which will help them connect with each other's feelings and physical reactions. This technique is directed at improving our perception so that we can better appreciate our magical companion as the objective of our enjoyment.

First, the lovers agree to exchange their sex roles. This is done by imitating the movements that your partner naturally makes or the position he or she usually takes during erotic play. Next, one will act out a role and the other will imitate it. This mirror imitation technique is used to learn any dance, not just in the bedroom.

During sexual acts, human beings can sample and learn different experiences, connecting themselves with creativity and pleasure. By practicing this exercise at least once per week, and then once a month, one can achieve astonishing results.

The partner that understands his or her own magical rhythm transforms sexuality in the true art of loving.

Explosive Orgasm

Every cubic inch of the human body constantly radiates its internal state of being. In return, every cubic inch of the body continually receives psychic input—feelings, thoughts, intentions, the general state of consciousness—from everyone it encounters. This process is automatic and unconscious.

Sexual excitement is also part of the internal state and can be provoked by various factors: involuntarily or unwittingly, or as the result of sexual fantasies and images, or by direct, stimulating physical contact.

Sexual relations should always be initiated in a conscious manner. When men are sexually stimulated, their bodies naturally release a substance that causes relaxation and the subsequent erection of the penis. Men should learn to maintain this state of relaxation so as to postpone ejaculation. Women experience better orgasms when men are able to maintain their erections longer.

To multiply the satisfaction of both partners, the first step is to concentrate on the whole body and begin to relax in order to generate the perfect chemistry. With practice, both lovers can sense that part every of the body feels different; in this way, you will discover that there is not any zone that cannot be intensely enjoyed through physical contact. When the skin is stimulated—with caresses, massages, or kisses—the body vibrates, like it is all one erogenous zone. This is the beginning of enriching the erotic experience. With the necessary techniques and knowledge of the body, both men and women can achieve multiple orgasms.

Sexual pleasure is unlimited when the mind is freed by the true knowledge of our sexual power. The orgasm mechanism can be explained as a liberating explosion of sexual energy. This explosion provokes muscular contractions all over the body and their subsequent relaxation. The frequency of these muscular contractions is caused by the contraction of the blood vessels, and lasts several seconds for both sexes.

Single Orgasm

This sexual and physiological discharge results in a moment of sexual pleasure lasting between two and ten seconds. Both sexes can induce it through masturbation without needing another person to participate.

Multiple Orgasms

This state of pleasure results when a partner has been sufficiently stimulated physically. The experience of each physical contraction multiples for women when done between two to ten second rests. For women, these orgasms can be continuous or dispersed.

Chains of Orgasms

A continuous chain or long sequence of single orgasms can result in six to a dozen climaxes. In the case of men, ejaculation only happens in the last of these orgasmic contractions. In women, ejaculation is also provoked only once and without hindering the release of pleasure. A woman can control a chain of orgasms, depending on when she wants to finish the erotic session. Control over the orgasm depends on psychological and emotional factors once the woman has achieved this maximum state of pleasure. To produce a chain of orgasms, the woman should be able to anticipate how long each orgasm or sexual relation will last.

Refractory Period

The refractory or recovery period after an orgasm is the time that the body needs to recuperate from the orgasmic discharge before returning to a state of arousal. In women, this phase can be about ten minutes long, according to the stimulation given by the magical partner. For men, this period lasts longer (between fourteen and twenty minutes) and depends on the motivation that their partner gives them as well as the man's age and physical condition.

Tactics for Being a Divine Companion

For men and women who desire perfection in the sensual art of loving, here are some essential characteristics for learning and practicing:

Confidence: Whatever your age, sex or social status, you need to demonstrate confidence in the art of making love, even though it may be your first time having sexual contact with someone.

Trust: It is fundamental to gain the trust of your partner when seducing him or her. You should feel more comfortable with your body than ever before. When fear or inhibition creates a sexual block, it hinders the final objective.

Perseverance: Tenacity demonstrates to our lover our intention to seduce him or her and to share our internal strength and energy. It is a way to convince them and to persuade them that the pleasure and enjoyment that they will feel is going to be sufficiently intense to remember it always.

Use your body. It is very important to nurture your partner's energy with your own body energy. Transferring energy through embracing and touching can enhance your own excitement and awaken you to the pleasure of the other.

Be intuitive. Not only should you utilize spoken language to seduce the other, it is also fundamental to develop your intuition and listen without words, or with your heart. That is how we will understand the more profound meaning of the mystery and the passionate event called love.

Be protective. It is an important step in erotic participation to make the desired person feel protected. This encourages intimacy, sweetness, and serenity in lovemaking.

Demonstrate power and magnetism. It can stimulate a lover to show him or her an unexpected strength or something about you that surprises them. Always be attentive to their tastes. A simple surprise gift can conquer and charm even the most stubborn or difficult of lovers.

The encounter with the desired one should always be a kind of celebration. But first, you have to understand all of their preferences and needs in order to identify what gives them happiness and joy.

With a balanced share of romanticism and eroticism, you will make every encounter incomparable.

The Secrets of Happiness

Accept yourself as you are. The body is a temple, a sacred place, where the universe is revered. You are a great mystery made up of many energies that combine in numerous dimensions. Accept it and move with each energy, with profound lucidity, love, and understanding. Then each desire will find its own way to manifest in reality. Happiness is not something that happens; it is the fruit of learning and experience. Nobody taught us the tools that generate this feeling.

What is Happiness? What Does it Mean to be Happy?

This mysterious question occurs to each of us, often early in life, when we discover that happiness is what everyone looks for and wants. In this way, social conditioning begins. As time passes, being happy often means finding your first love, graduating from college, getting married, having children, getting a new house, or sometimes getting a divorce.

But in reality, these great moments have always been the result of taking big risks and making big sacrifices. When it comes time to enjoy the life we've built, very few people can do it fully.

The Happy Choice

Happiness is not something that happens to us; it is something that we accept, in whatever moment of our lives, regardless of what is happening around us. Happiness is the natural state of one's soul. Happiness is a life choice, a personal disposition, liberation, an ability to focus our energy and attention on loving ourselves, helping ourselves and releasing ourselves from all pain.

What do we have to do to feel this way?

Start a happiness campaign. Get a notebook to plan your life. Draw a happy face on every page. Write the words happiness, smile, joy, and so on in every language you know. Then you should make corresponding notes. On the left hand page, write questions or objectives, and on the right hand page put the answers.

Exercise: Life Plan

First step: Dedicate the first page to rewarding yourself and thanking the people that help you achieve your personal wishes.

Second step: Make a list of all the things you do to be happy. On another list, write what you do (purposely or not) that results in unhappiness. Explore which behaviors cloud your happiness.

Ask yourself what you want in life, what you wish to achieve, your life goals. Ask your heart.

Third step: Assess your emotional life. Do this with sincerity and set aside ample time to do it without interruptions. The most important thing is to discover which thoughts block and which ones facilitate happiness.

Ten Revelations for Being Happy

1. Faith creates trust, gives us mental peace, and frees the soul from doubt.

2. Our attitudes can change us; this is how we change the world. The only things that can change the world are our thoughts and intentions.

3. It is important to exercise and take care of one's body. Physical conditioning reduces stress and generates the secretion of endorphins.

4. Learn to live for the here and now.

5. Set objectives and work toward them. A goal is a dream with a concrete date for achieving it.

6. Smile—it improves self-esteem. When we smile, our brain understands it as a signal that everything is all right.

7. Cultivate forgiveness: As long as we resent and hate, it will be impossible to be happy.

8. Gratitude provides faith and strength every day.

9. Develop your personal relationships. Working together, we can accomplish great things.

10. Love helps us give and receive small and large joys.

The more you live in your heart, the more opportunity you will have to live in this world happily.

Next, we will explore the unconscious mind and utilize its magic in becoming divine lovers.

I dreamt of paradise, your eyes were the sky, your
hug, the earth. Your sweat was the water,
your passion the fire.
I dreamt that our dreams united, our souls met and
our hearts touched.
Maybe a strange fairy spell, wizards
and elves will teach me the formula to follow
dreaming with you for eternity…

Mabel Jam

Chapter 9

Dreams and Their Meanings

Since the beginning of time, human beings have been fascinated by dreams. In Egypt, dreams had vital importance. Priests specialized in their interpretation and consulted them before taking any important action. The Greeks thought that dreams were messages from the gods, and thus attributed a great deal of importance to them.

Many philosophical and psychological theories about dreams developed through the ages. One theory states that the soul knows the past-life history and present-life background of each person and that it reveals this knowledge, which is hidden from our waking mind, with symbols and images in our dreams. Interpreting these sometimes mysterious messages has been an important part of magic in every culture.

We have already explained the importance of the unconscious mind in erotic magic. We must use the unconscious in a conscious way through the act of dreaming; the purpose is to understand ourselves better and to achieve a deep spiritual relationship with our magical partner.

When the light is turned off and we are in bed, our mind is set free. The desires and fears that we cannot acknowledge when we are awake are open to us.

What are the real desires and the real needs of a person? How do we improve our life when we are not satisfied with it? The answers lie within our dreams.

Dreaming is a creative activity that happens at the deepest level of one's mind. How can we explain all those interrelated scenes that come from our unknown and hidden levels of conscience? Those images are symbols that our soul uses to express our most intimate desires, secret hopes, and hidden fears.

During our dreams, our thoughts and desires become objectives and those fabricated scenes become real; sometimes they seem much more real than the scenes we live when we are awake.

The Sleep Process

While dreaming, the body relaxes and the mind drifts away from the realities of the world that surrounds us, while our vital bodily functions continue uninterrupted. Scientific studies using electroencephalograms show a marked change in the intensity of brain waves as we sleep and dream. Every night we have four or five cycles of sleep that last between seventy and a hundred minutes. In each of them, we go through three stages: the lucid stage, light sleep, and deep or REM (Rapid Eye Movement) sleep.

The first stage of sleep is known as the lucid phase. Premonitory dreams usually happen at the beginning of our sleep or just before waking up because our conscious mind is more alert.

During this stage, our respiration changes, blood pressure increases, and the brain shows activity as if we were awake. This explains why many people realize that they are dreaming but they cannot wake up, even if they try to do so. If the dreamer awakes or is awakened during this stage, it is much easier for him or her to remember the dream. But each instant that passes distorts the content of the dream. For this reason, we recommend that you write down the experience as soon as possible afterward.

Connecting to Our True Self

In the stage of light sleep—the middle point where our external consciousness is less likely to wake us up—our body is more relaxed and it can enter into real contact with our higher Self. The soul can leave the body in a conscious or unconscious way. If we want to follow it, we can use certain techniques that will help us make that journey. Before we embark, we must prepare ourselves. It is important that we ingest a very light meal that evening, preferably a vegetarian meal. Our sleep clothing should be loose and comfortable, made of natural fibers. The room must have a pleasant temperature and be completely silent. Some people like to submerge themselves in a lukewarm saltwater bath before retiring. This is not necessary, but it can help free energetic blockages in the body.

Exercise: Journey to the Future

After the physical relaxation, perform a creative visualization with slow and controlled breathing. The idea is to find a master teacher or guide within ourselves. His or her image may be very real or familiar. This master or wise person will take us on a journey within our own soul to a place where we can learn something about the future or something about ourselves.

We could:
- Discover how to improve our relationship with our magical partner
- Discover how to improve our erotic ability
- Recognize some personal characteristics that we may want to change

Then we surrender to our dreams, repeating to ourselves what we want to find out, for example: "I am going to remember my dream clearly and I am going to understand it."

This technique can also be used in conjunction with meditation exercises without any need to sleep, but it is easier through our dreams.

Different Types of Dreams

Dreams with Emotional Content

These are dreams caused by our internal tensions: unsatisfied or conflicted desires, frustrated hopes, and multiple fears that lurk in our soul like the fear of death, insecurity, solitude, failure, and so on.

These stressful emotions sometimes result in nightmares. Their purpose is to remind us that our inner world has been neglected and needs attention. Everyday events often demand so much of our energy that we are unable to stay centered and in touch with our deepest needs. We could say that the unconscious mind reveals images in the form of nightmares so that we can take action to avoid living those situations in our real life.

Clear or Lucid Dreams

These dreams are particularly vivid and are marked by the person being aware of the dream in present tense while dreaming it. They spring from the wealth of our personal unconscious and the collective unconscious.

Premonitory Dreams

A form of extrasensory perception wherein we dream about a specific future event or situation that eventually comes to pass in reality. The unconscious mind is where our inner wisdom lies. At this mental level, time does not exist as we know it, but rather, all becomes an eternal present. Thus our soul sometimes will let us know about certain experiences, positive or not, in the form of a dream.

Mystical Dreams

These dreams come from our soul; the unconscious mind acts according to the inner evolution of the dreamer. They are scenes, events and situations that reveal recurrent worries or beliefs with respect to ethical, moral or religious problems, and/or our spiritual life. Symbols related to a particular faith or religious belief such as angels, saints, or mystical signs are often included.

Erotic Dreams

Erotic dreams in particular do not always relate logically to our everyday life and waking emotions. They may be violent, exaggerated, embarrassing, or perverted, and they usually relate to intimate sexual conflicts and emotional needs that are hidden in the remote places of our unconscious.

Erotic dreams may be scary, frustrating, or pleasurable. From the content of the dream we can evaluate the degree of emotional repression on the part of the dreamer, and dreams can reveal latent violence—either conscious or denied by that person—that cannot be channeled in his or her life. Dreams can also reveal the wide range of sexual possibilities that the dreamer may enjoy.

Among other things, erotic dreams may reveal fear of intimacy. They are very common during adolescence or in persons who experience sexual abstinence.

Female Erotic Dreams

A survey in the United States showed that about seventy percent of the women interviewed had had erotic dreams at some point in their lives. A high percentage said they had had orgasms during an erotic dream. This survey also showed that women tend to have erotic dreams before menstruation, during ovulation, and during pregnancy—times that are marked by changes in the level of hormones. Women who have erotic dreams usually have less sexual activity in their lives. It is common for women with sexual inhibitions to have dreams about being violated or experiencing sexual harassment by strangers.

When a woman has a more active sexual life, she may dream about a person she knows or a person she has fantasies about, and she can have very pleasurable erotic experiences during those dreams.

Male Erotic Dreams

A man may have fantasies and erotic dreams about passionate, uninhibited women who desire him deeply and are ready to fulfill his most risky sexual fantasies. It is common for men to dream about sex with multiple partners, or about total sexual dominance toward women they fantasize about or women they cannot conquer.

When a man dreams about a homosexual relationship, it is probable that he is actually rejecting that idea. This may be because of fears or repressed needs in his daily life that threaten his masculine identity.

When men, especially teenagers, have an erotic dream, they may ejaculate several times in their sleep. These events can be studied to determine the level of impotence in some men. The erections during sleep are used to discount biological factors in the majority of the cases.

Sexual magic attempts to interpret dreams to obtain self-knowledge and to deepen the magical couple's bond. It is believed that couples can even reach a sexual connection through their dreams.

Exercise: Erotic Connection

During the first phase of sleep, our body is in a quiet state of vigil. Our unconscious Self is most accessible at the beginning of our sleep and when we begin to wake up. It is important to establish contact with it so as to have access to the information and wisdom found when dreaming begins.

It is possible to learn how to transfer messages from our unconscious to our conscious mind, and to resolve conflicts through our dreams. To achieve this, practice some creative visualization techniques (see chapter 5) before falling asleep. You can do this as a couple or alone.

If doing this exercise as a couple, it is very important that each of you pay attention to the motives or desires that your magical partner expresses in the dreams. It is also important to establish the objective that you want to transmit through the erotic dream, and how it could be achieved in a conscious way. If done individually, write about the results of this experience in your notebook.

After achieving relaxation, concentrate on the person with whom you want to be united. Allow your unconscious mind to discover the sexual or emotional conflicts that prevent you from fulfilling that connection.

After this exercise, repeat the following affirmation:

I, (your name), will connect with the superior Self of (name of the other person) during our sleep, and I will understand and remember the dream. Tomorrow, when I wake up, I will write it down in detail.

Once you understand the reason for the conflict, you will understand the real physical or emotional problems, which is the first step toward creating a more open relationship. The idea behind connecting with the superior Self of another person is to avoid a telepathic distortion in that person's dream due to the projection of your own desires.

Some people wonder if they have had an astral voyage in their sleep when they dream of the other person. The answer is usually no; they have simply searched the archives of the unconscious for all the knowledge that the superior Self can communicate to the conscious mind.

Symbology and Meaning of Our Dreams

Dreams open the door to the mystery of our inner world. If you want to know yourself better, the answers are in your dreams. When we learn how to interpret our dreams, we can better understand our hidden emotions. This not only helps us take the steps needed to manifest our desires in reality, it also improves the flow of energy throughout our body.

The dream language works through symbols and images, memories, experiences, customs, and deep emotions that rest at our unconscious level. To interpret our dreams we must approach them with a relaxed mind, free of preconceptions, and try to avoid rational suggestions and explanations. Occasionally the dream means exactly what it seems to reveal, but each image hides something we must uncover and decipher to reach the real message. It is extremely important to take note of all our dreams to be able to reach a more advanced and accurate interpretation. With practice, you will acquire a feel for how your own unconscious mind presents its messages. For interpretations of some common dream symbols and situations, please see the Appendix on page 145.

We are somewhat more than our selves in our sleeps, and the slumber of the body seems to be but the waking of the soul. It is the ligation of sense, but the liberty of reason; and our waking conceptions do not match the Fancies of our sleeps.

Thomas Browne

Conclusion

The Magic of Love Fulfills Your Dreams

This book has given you all the practical and theoretical tools needed to achieve authentic freedom about sex. You should understand how to preserve harmony between your inner world and your relationship with the external world, as you practice responsibility and freedom in achieving pleasure. Enjoy each experience as a game of energies that flow constantly; enjoy the present while trusting the message of your heart.

These are the principles that help us to become divine lovers:

Love, nurture, and protect your body.

Know your whole body like a map to promote mutual satisfaction.

Trust and listen to your body language during an erotic encounter.

Understand your inner world.

Be alert to all types of signals that your partner gives you in a sexual relationship.

Understand, without judging, the sexual fantasies that come from your inner self.

Respect the desires, beliefs, and ideas of others.

Be open to enjoy new experiences with your partner, being totally committed to the true needs of both of you.

Find new information and renew your knowledge about other techniques to achieve pleasure.

Understand that erotic contact is a fascinating exchange between two persons.

Maintain sexual ethics with your partner. Respect the privacy and parameters you agree upon for each new encounter.

Observe what your partner does not like.

When suggesting a type of sexual communication, don't impose rules that are not shared by your partner.

Respect the sexual fantasies and tendencies of others, even if you do not participate in them or agree with them.

Continually seek to renew and re-energize the erotic aspect of your life, regardless of how long the relationship has lasted.

Find free time where you can create total harmony.

Be more conscious of your possibilities and limitations.

Develop coherence between your feelings, beliefs, and thoughts and act accordingly.

Enjoy every single instant of every erotic encounter with your partner, being aware that it is a unique moment that cannot be repeated.

Find satisfaction with your partner in a natural and fluid way.

Be open to giving and receiving emotional and sexual satisfaction in each encounter.

Evaluate the content of your erotic dreams to try to discover their
unconscious message.

Find divinity in your partner and within yourself.

Now you have the opportunity to practice all these principles and
techniques; practice them every day to grow and develop your love. This
way, you will be able to create a world without sexual or spiritual blockages. If you can create a new world, it is because you understand that
you are the universe and that your being is the most sacred place where
you can live forever.

Appendix

Dream Dictionary

A

ABANDONMENT: This is a frequent dream with a variety of subtle meanings. First you must distinguish between being abandoned yourself and abandoning someone or something. If someone abandons you, the dream may show your fear of not being accepted from a sexual or emotional point of view by your partner. If you are abandoned by a very powerful person, the dream indicates the possibility of being free from someone's erotic or emotional dominance. If you are abandoned by your lover, it may reveal a hidden desire to end the relationship, or a fear of the relationship ending. If it is your partner who abandons you, you may fear the results of your own actions.

When you abandon someone or something, you are living a life tied to outdated customs or principles, or perhaps you feel trapped by an environment, family or friends that hinder your potential. Whatever you abandon in this dream will symbolize the reasons for your imprisonment, and so you will realize what you must modify or release. Some dreams about abandonment may also indicate a warning about your health.

ABBEY: If you see religious buildings in your dream, that is a sign of intellectual, moral, or spiritual doubts, or concerns with respect to your present love relationship. Your attitude about the abbey will reveal the intensity and the focus of those concerns. If you walk in front of the abbey but do not enter it, this means that your concerns are not yet defined. If you enter the abbey, it means that you already know your concerns and are looking for answers. If you pray in the abbey, your desires will become a reality and bring happiness.

ABBOT, ABBESS: May refer to erotic repression. See also priest.

ABDICATION: Recognize that you may be exercising too much control over your dependents, be it at work or at home. Try not to be so dominant and give more freedom to others, or you will risk losing it all.

ABORTION, SPONTANEOUS (miscarriage): This is a common dream in pregnant women. Even if there are no physical signs of a potential abortion, you should see a doctor or a gynecologist for an examination. Dreaming of an abortion that affects you personally is a premonition of something that will not have a happy ending, or that you will suffer a cruel deception. If you see a woman who is aborting and you assist her, you may suffer a serious illness, wound, or accident. If you simply observe it without getting involved, your projects may suffer delays for unpredictable reasons. Common symbols that may relate to abortion include red running water, a runaway horse or an aggressive horse, a tortoise belly-up or a dead chicken.

ABSCESS: In a dream, the person with an abscess has or will have emotional problems with someone. The degree of maturation of the abscess indicates the evolution of that problem. If the abscess is hard and has not matured, the problem has not reached its end. If it is matured and open, the emotional problem is about to be solved. If you are the one who has the abscess, you may be coming into or ending a period of problems or bad luck; the stage of the abscess will show whether you are at the beginning or near its end.

ABSOLUTION: If you are absolved by a person, a tribunal, or an institution, there will soon be a favorable change in someone's attitude toward you. The circumstances in the dream will determine the degree of importance.

ABSTAIN: A deep deception is waiting for you.

ABUNDANCE: You are living under a false security; a difficult situation may be approaching in which your resources may be diminished or compromised.

ABYSS: If you fall into an abyss, you are about to end a situation due to a weakness in your way of life. You must change the situation and adjust accordingly. If you fall into an abyss but you can get out of it, or if you have to cross it via an unstable bridge, there is the possibility that you can fix that situation and achieve happiness again, but only after many difficulties. If you see the abyss but you do not fall into it, then you still have time to avoid the harm that is threatening you.

ACCELERATING: Be careful with your emotional outbursts since they may be harmful.

ACCIDENT: The dream indicates fear of important decisions and stressful situations. Analyze whether you feel some insecurity about your ability to control your reflexes and emotions. Otherwise, the dream means that your personal, professional, or social future will face an important obstacle. If you escape the accident, your common sense will help you get out of an embarrassing situation. If you witness the accident, your life will be affected by humiliation or misfortune.

ACCLAIM: If you are honored or praised during a dream but you cannot see the faces of those who are praising you (or those faces do not have any meaning for you), that is a sign of danger, and almost always danger caused by letting yourself be dragged down by base passions.

ACCOUNTANT: Some aspects of your life need to be put in order. If you are the accountant, it may show fear of financial problems, or fear of having to account for yourself.

ACCUMULATE: If you accumulate money in your dream, you may be at risk of losing money in real life. If you accumulate objects, it may symbolize upcoming discomforts or entrapment.

ACCUSATIONS: If you are accused of something, it indicates that you will avoid a trap and that your general outlook will be happy. If you see an accused person, or if you accuse someone, then it announces problems, sadness, and worries.

ACID: Forecasts fights or deceptions in the near future.

ACROBAT, ACROBATICS: Seeing an acrobat performing or seeing oneself doing the acrobatics indicates that in real life you are facing an unstable situation that will have the same outcome as your dream. If you are doing the acrobatics and it feels nice, that means your independence and security will be fortified by your present relationship. If the activity is not pleasant, or if there are mistakes in the acrobatics, then that unstable situation may not end favorably, or you will have failures or financial losses.

ACTOR, ACTRESS: If you are acting, it means that you will know how to find success in a present enterprise related to love or work. If the dream is recurrent, you cannot resolve some problems that are bothering you. If you see other people acting, be wary of frivolous pleasures or untrustworthy friends that may take advantage of you.

ADMIRATION: If you feel admiration for something or someone, there may be a person with hidden motives who is trying to influence you. If you feel admired, you may have too high an opinion of yourself.

ADOLESCENTS: If you are an adult without a romantic partner and you dream about adolescents of the opposite sex, it indicates that you may have trouble finding a spouse, as you are looking for perfection that does not exist.

ADOPTION: If you adopt another person, maybe your unconscious is saying that you lack purpose in life. If you are adopted, then it may show lack of affection or need for protection and support. It may also mean responsibilities affecting people who should not be affected by them.

AILMENTS: If you feel ill or you are seriously affected by the ailment in your dream, you should consult with your doctor since your health may be in danger. But if the dream does not show any sign of something unpleasant and it is in fact pleasing, then it means financial success. If you see one or more ailing persons in your dream, some of your projects may suffer delays or upsets.

AIRPLANE: Flying on a plane represents a pleasant sexual relationship; if the airplane cannot take off, it may indicate impotency. If the plane crashes, it may mean feelings of insecurity in your present relationship. May also represent rapid elevation to a higher social, professional, or spiritual status.

AIRPORT: If there is a lot of activity with planes coming and going, the dream announces a time of great change, with issues, things, or people that come and go. You may also see airport scenes after a long illness or a long painful period.

ALMONDS: Bitter almonds may be an omen of family fights or disagreements with older people. If the almond is in the shell and hard to crack, it may represent your unconscious. You will have to overcome many problems to achieve your goals.

ALTAR: If you appear in front of an altar with a person of the opposite sex, the dream suggests sexual attraction. If the people are of the same sex, then it alludes to homosexual fantasies.

AMPUTATION: This may be interpreted simply as a period of losses, but often it reflects fear of impotency, or in a wider sense, the fear to love or be loved.

ANCHOR: Weighing or raising an anchor means you are still searching for your true home, but commitments constantly hinder you. You need to find your place.

ANGEL: One of the most positive dreams you can have involves seeing angels or other celestial beings; it signals an end to your problems. In a spiritual sense, the dream means to surrender to a Supreme Being. If the angels are sad, angry or seem to be threatening, the dreams is reflecting your fears or worries.

ANTS: Need to tend to organized work and planning ahead.

ANVIL: An omen of work and profits when you hammer an anvil in your dream. If you are a man, you need to take a more active role in your relationship. If you are a woman, you need to express any sexual dissatisfaction you feel.

APRON: Symbolizes work. If the apron is clean, you are being professional and effective. If it is dirty, the dream may announce problems and disagreements at work.

AQUARIUM: Seeing an aquarium with fishes swimming peacefully is a sign of tranquility and enduring happiness.

AQUEDUCT: You will take a long business trip; its outcome is dependent upon the condition of the aqueduct. If it is in good condition, you will achieve most of your goals. If it is in bad repair, a financial deception may result.

ARK: You need to overcome your doubts and make a decision.

ARMOR: Indicates that you either have or need protection. The general state of the armor will provide clues about the situation.

ARMY: Worry about an impending problem. The circumstances of the dream and the condition of the army reflect the resources you have to confront the problem.

ARROW: An arrow flying through the air suggests idealism. If you shoot the arrow, it means that you desire to be unconventional in your personal life.

ARTICHOKE: A symbol of persistence in pursuing someone you desire.

ASCENDING: Indicates courage, determination, and persistence that will help you achieve important personal goals.

ATTORNEY: If the attitude of the lawyer is favorable toward you, then you are on your way to resolving the conflict the dream represents. If his or her attitude is negative, you may need to change your approach. If the attorney is dealing with someone besides you, a friend may need your help.

B

BABY: Represents creativity and new beginnings. You may start a new business or project soon, or your abilities will be recognized.

BAG: A closed bag represents small secrets that you want to keep from others. If you lose the bag, it means you fear to let anyone know you intimately.

BANDITS: Represent the forces of the unconscious; the control of these forces signifies a greater capacity for success over everyday problems.

BANQUET: If you are one of the persons invited, it may reveal your desire to have access to an environment in which you do not belong, a place ruled by conventions and appearances. Eating a lot at the banquet symbolizes the desires you are trying to satisfy.

BAREFOOT: Reflects your own feelings of weakness or poverty, not necessarily material. You feel helpless in the circumstances that surround you.

BATTLE: If you observe the battle from a distance, you want to change your situation and organize it in a different way. If you are participating in the battle or preparing for battle, you are facing obstacles in achieving your goals.

BEACH: If it is crowded, the dream indicates a need to show off and have new social relationships. If the beach is empty, it implies the desire for peace and tranquility. If the beach is dirty, it shows the need to order your mind and feelings.

BEARD: If you trim your beard, the moment has come to take direct and voluntary action about something that worries you. If you let your beard grow, it is a warning to moderate your excessive desire for power and honor. If there is a barber in the dream, you can count on the assistance of very important people.

BED: The dream signifies the attitudes you have toward your own sexuality and your partner. A clean and/or ornamental bed represents your desire to improve your romantic relationship. A broken bed reflects problems in your relationship, while a dirty or untidy bed shows you feel uncomfortable about the relationship or your partner.

BEES: Bees are a symbol of erotic love; if you see bees on a flower, it is a sign of a new love. Bees also predict success and prosperity due to hard work and team work. If the bees make honey at your home or property, success and fortune are guaranteed. If you are stung by a bee, it means that your reputation is at risk due to slander. If you see bees attacking you, the dream reflects conflicts with your associates, or shows that you will abandon your work in search of pleasure. This may bring misfortune and loss of wealth. If the bees enter your home, office or business, it is a sign of success or having an advantage over the competition. If you destroy a beehive, then you may cause labor problems—you will suffer some harm.

BEGGAR (or VAGABOND): If you are the beggar, it announces that you are entering a difficult period, with problems and lots of work that will not bring you much benefit.

BENDING: It may be a sign of low self-esteem, or it may indicate that a problem has been too much for you and you would like someone else to take on that responsibility.

BET: You may be leaving too many things to chance, and fear losses due to your lack of caution.

BICYCLE: If you see a bicycle pass by, your dream is suggesting that your youth is passing you by. If you ride the bicycle, it indicates a desire for freedom.

BIRDS: Seeing or listening to birds is a symbol of good luck. Multicolored birds almost always symbolize people who have a superior psychological level and who will teach you and protect you. Black or ugly birds refer to negative or destructive thoughts or fantasies. A flying songbird signifies the arrival of good times in your love relationship. If the bird descends abruptly, you may face emotional disappointments. If the bird is standing on the ground, you must be very prudent when you act. A flock of birds coming toward you at high speed is a warning of a threat. If the birds attack you, your negative thoughts or the negative thoughts of other people are affecting you. If you catch a bird alive, this is a good time to take advantage of an opportunity. If you kill any birds in your dream, you will have problems and go through a stage of stagnation. If you kill them in self-defense, you will receive satisfaction despite your struggles.

BLINDNESS: This may indicate you are acting without considering all the possibilities or points of view; stop and reflect before proceeding. May also symbolize an illogical fear of being betrayed or persecuted, or a feeling of helplessness.

BLOOD: May be a warning about circulatory problems, but also the feeling that life escapes without us noticing it. Sorrow or depression that reduces your vitality.

BLUE: Blue relates to harmony, tranquility, devotion, and good health. If you are materialistic, it may be a warning about a threat or risk to your financial security. People with great intuition, psychic powers or extrasensory perception often see this color in their dreams.

BOARD: This is a good time to change strategies and make plans.

BOAT (or SHIP): Almost always relates to one's love relationship or social relationships. Pay attention to the condition of the boat and how it navigates.

BOATMAN: This dream is related to the mythical archetype of death, and it may indicate emotional conflicts. The interpretation depends on your participation in relation to the boat. If you see the boat leave, it represents distance and farewells. Seeing the boat arrive may refer to something you are expecting.

BONES: Broken bones mean feelings of impotency or diminished sexuality. Can also be interpreted as loss of hope or depression.

BOOK: A closed book symbolizes a part of your life that you want to keep hidden. If the books are dusty or scattered, it means you have too many projects to finish. The title of the book may help interpret your dream.

BOREDOM: Difficulties or worries may be coming and it will be hard to overcome them if you cannot discover the reason for your inner boredom as revealed in the dream.

BOTTLE: Full bottles generally mean prosperity, especially if they are wine bottles. If the bottle is full of something very valuable or something you like, it announces a great surprise. If it is empty, it may predict an illness due to lack of energy or a weakened immune system. Broken, dirty, or discarded bottles forecast problems at home in the near future.

BOTTOM: The bottom of any ordinary object in a dream indicates that this is a good time to investigate the unknown and search out other people's true motives.

BRAKES: If you see yourself using the brakes, the dream may reflect insecurity on your part, a fear to go too far or too fast.

BREAK, BREAKING: This is a stage in which you need to examine the deep issues in your subconscious so you can release old burdens.

BREASTS: Represent the instinct to feed or nurture. Only in an erotic dream do breasts relate to a sexual need, especially for a woman.

BUMBLEBEE: A sign that somebody is trying to cause you harm. If you work in agriculture, tend your crops without missing a detail. If you kill any bumblebees in the dream, then you will discover the traps that threaten you.

BUNDLE: To carry a bundle means you are facing a situation that affects your mood. If someone picks up your bundle, it reflects your desire to avoid facing a problem.

BURNS: May refer to a love wound that you should heal; may also be a warning about fire and hot surfaces.

BUS: May show an unconscious need for more sexual activity, or sexual group fantasies. It is important to determine who is taking part in the dream and analyze their reactions to the events.

BUTTER: A symbol of security and trust in your financial situation. If you see yourself beating the butter, it announces an inheritance or a birth in the family. Eating butter is a warning to prepare for a great physical effort.

BUTTERFLY: Symbol of the soul and psyche, it suggests transformation and spiritual awakening. It heralds a radical internal change, a metamorphosis, the ability to rise above the solely material aspects of life.

C

CAGE: Represents isolation and limitation. You must consider the reasons you withdraw into yourself.

CALENDAR: If you see a specific date, it may indicate the need to make a decision. If you only see the calendar, you may be wasting your time on unimportant issues.

CAMEL: Seeing or riding one signals that you have a strong will that will help you triumph over difficulties that may be approaching. If the camel is in the desert, then you are already facing those difficulties.

CAPTURE: If you capture insects or animals, it symbolizes a situation or an issue that is getting out of your control. If you capture an enemy, you feel subjugated by that person in waking life.

CAR: Symbolizes our own humanity, and may also reflect one's ambition and desire for power. An accident may forecast an illness caused by too much haste, not necessarily in an automobile.

CARDS: Indicates risk and may be a warning to use all your strength and will to control the events.

CAT: The cat is a symbol of sensibility and intuition. If the cat rubs against you, it means a woman wants something from you. If you feed the cat, or if it scratches you, it means rivalry among lovers. Black cats may be interpreted as repressed sensuality or eroticism, while white cats mean weakness of character or indecisiveness. Golden cats are good luck, and tiger-striped cats symbolize the fortitude to do things on your own.

CATASTROPHE: A desire for drastic change in some situation, or the need to clarify events.

CAVE: Caves represent earth energy and may also indicate a need for protection. If you go inside the cave, it symbolizes the need to get to know yourself better, or to analyze something in detail. If you get lost in the cave, it is a symbol of confusion. If you see yourself coming out of the cave, it shows you making decisions and proceeding toward your goals.

CEILING BEAMS: Symbolize support from those close to you; represents security if it is a solid beam and fear if it is weak.

CHAIN: Almost always refers to your past causing consequences in the present. The anchor-chain of a boat means you are still tied to a previous situation, while breaking the chain represents a conclusion to your worries or problems.

CHAIR: If you are sitting on it, the dream refers to security and the beginning of a stable period.

CHEESE: If you buy it, there may be some deceit, or you may be in contact with people who are not very sincere. Indicates emotional upsets.

CHERUB: Symbolizes spiritual protection and indicates a period of good luck, especially in love.

CHESS: Even though dreams that show strategic games are good omens for happiness and friendship, the game of chess indicates that you have a problem and do not dare take the action you are contemplating.

CHICKEN: Considered a sign of confusion and disorder. Do not pay attention to gossips or rumors.

CHOCOLATE: Represents sensual pleasures. If you eat the chocolate it means a declaration of love or achieving deep sexual satisfaction.

CLARIFICATION: The meaning of a suspicious event or situation will become clear.

CLAWS: If you see claw-like hands, you are expressing an emotional need to hold on to your partner.

CLIFF: You will face difficulties now or in the future; their degree will be shown by your proximity to a dangerous cliff. If you are climbing the cliff, in spite of all the difficulties that may arise, you can be sure of a successful outcome.

CLOSET: Represents your most intimate passions, your cultural heritage, or your creativity. The contents of the closet, and whether you open or close the door, may suggest your attitude towards a problem.

CLOUDS: Symbolize sentimentalism, worries, and unclear circumstances. The intensity of those worries or circumstances may be assessed by the appearance of the clouds. The darker and stormier the clouds, the worse the situation.

COAL (or CHARCOAL): Burning coals represent passion, usually of a sexual nature. If you see coal that is not burning, it may indicate your desire to put a project into motion, but you are considering each step you should take. If you see smoke, a situation is becoming too complex emotionally and you should slow down.

COAT: If you wear a coat, you may be hiding your true personality. If another person wears the coat, someone close to you who is hiding selfish intentions under a false façade.

COCKROACH: Represents a particular problem you need to take care of in a decisive way.

COFFEE: If you make the coffee, it represents great happiness at home or in your relationship; erotic desires can be fulfilled for both partners. Toasting coffee beans may signal an unexpected visitor or the visit of someone you would like to see. Growing or harvesting coffee beans suggests you will receive awards or great wealth.

COFFIN: Erotic fantasies are deeply repressed. If the coffin is open, it means that you feel threatened by events from your past. If closed, it may be interpreted as a desire to hide something you do not like.

COLD: Generally represents solitude, sadness, or a lack of progress. If you are protecting yourself from the cold, it means that even if you see that a situation is stagnant, you must be patient so as to stop the negative influences.

COMFORTER: A thick comforter, comfy and warm, may indicate a desire for security and protection. You may find it hard to confront difficulties in an independent way.

CONSTRUCTION: Represents your material possessions and ambitions. If the construction is large and solidly built, you will have the opportunity to expand your interests. If the buildings are small, your enterprise will be modest. If what you built is in bad condition, you should reconsider your plans. If you see public buildings, your ambitions are not in line with your abilities; you are at risk of suffering deception and failure if you do not alter your plans.

CONTAMINATION: Symbolizes fear and worries. You may feel unprotected or at a disadvantage in an important situation.

COOKIES: Suggests good health and small benefits. If you eat the cookie, it means pleasant news or visits. If you prepare the cookies, you want to make new friends.

CORAL: If you harvest coral from the bottom of the sea, the dream is indicating an extraordinary gain, but it requires some effort and risk. If you give away the coral, or if somebody gives it to you, it symbolizes lies and insincerity in a relationship.

CORK: Do not underestimate your enemies though they may appear insignificant. There is a risk of obstacles to your plans.

CORPSE: A symbol of loss, sadness, and the end of something. If you see yourself as the corpse, it indicates that you desire to escape from a situation or problem. If the corpse is an enemy, the dream symbolizes a bad conscience. If you assist at a wake or funeral, it shows you are ready to put some old struggles to rest.

CRAB: The dream shows your fear of getting involved in a particular situation or relationship. Indecision is making you lose ground. New job opportunities may be beyond your capabilities and you do not how to deal with them.

CRACK: An issue or situation is growing more complex. A relationship may be showing signs of cracking.

CRICKET: A herald of happiness and prosperity.

CROW: This is an omen of envy and gossip.

CURSE: You are in a rebellious stage and should stop to think about the underlying reasons for your negative feelings.

CURVES: The dream represents some type of defiance; you do not want to accept events as they are and are trying to shift your circumstances.

CUSTOMS OFFICE: May refer to an upcoming inspection or test. If you are in charge of the customs office, you are trying to impose your opinions on others. This is a typical dream during times of important life events such as in marriage, job change, moving, and so on. The dream may help you discover the hopes or fears you have about the situation.

D

DAISIES: White daisies are considered a promise of love, full of innocence and without expectations. May also mean indecision in sentimental matters.

DANCE: Symbolizes conflicts, either emotional or sexual, that you feel you cannot control. If you are in love, it may symbolize happiness and the fulfillment of desires. If you see yourself dancing and enjoying it, the dream it is a good omen for your success in love. If you dance in a costume it indicates that to have success with your partner, you need to be sincere. If you fall or if you trip, take this as a warning about wrong attitudes in your relationship. If the dream is unpleasant, there is a conflict between what you want and what you actually have.

DARKNESS: Symbolizes fears, worries, and the unknown.

DART: If you throw a dart, you are exercising your ambition and trying to influence others. If someone throws a dart at you, it means you feel trapped.

DATE: If the person is late to arrive, if he or she arrives with someone different from the person you were expecting, or if he or she never shows up, the dream symbolizes unattainable desires, disappointments, or indecision.

DEAFNESS: This indicates your desire not to hear, perhaps in reference to some advice you received.

DEATH: Dreaming of death does not announce physical death; it simply shows that something has died or disappeared. It may refer to a love relationship, a friendship, or a situation.

DEBTS: A desire to reach an agreement, a guilty conscience, or a fear of not being able to fulfill your commitments.

DECAPITATE: The head usually symbolizes our soul and intelligence. If you see yourself without a head, it means loss of position, either socially or emotionally.

DEFEAT: May be a warning to strengthen your will and self-reliance. Perhaps you have accepted defeat too easily.

DEFECATE: Freeing yourself from your problems. However, if you do this in an improper place, it represents complications.

DEW: Has a sacred connotation as it is the precursor of a new day. This is one of the best omens of good luck and fertility.

DICE: A symbol of chance that may be interpreted as a warning that you are letting yourself be controlled by events.

DIRT: This indicates that something is not right in relation to the object, person, or place involved. It is an invitation to have a cleansing cure, to wash yourself well, and it even suggests doing a good house cleaning.

DISGUISE: You may have difficulties accepting reality. You do not like a situation the way it is and would like to change it, but you are afraid to confront those involved.

DOG: Indicate a great desire to be loved and protected, and a desire for a partner who gives you unconditional love. If you see a dog in danger, it is a sign that some emotional relationship may be in danger.

DOLPHIN: A symbol of salvation that means you are on a good path, be it material or spiritual. If you see two dolphins, one pointing up and the other down, the dream symbolizes the double cosmic current of evolution and involution. If they are facing each other, it symbolizes the balance of feminine and masculine energies within oneself.

DOOR: If the door is opened and you see something pleasant, it means success. If you see yourself on the other side of the door, it means something unpleasant; perhaps you are not on the right path. If the door is closed, some issues will not materialize. It the door is the door to your home, pay attention to its condition; if it is ugly or in bad condition, it is time to be careful. If you observe many doors, you must make a decision.

DRAGON: The dragon is the symbol of wisdom and long life, but it also represents an internal struggle to overcome evil and the ignorance we all carry inside ourselves.

DRESSED UP: If you dream about people who are very well dressed or wear a lot of make-up, the dream is a warning that some of your friends or acquaintances may be insincere. If you are the person wearing the make-up, you will be forced to hide your true emotions or thoughts, or you will voluntarily try to cheat or commit treason. The atmosphere and the outcome of the dream will indicate which possibility is more fitting.

DRINKING: If you are drinking in happy surroundings, especially if you are drinking wine, the dream predicts happiness and contentment. The cup or glass is also important; if it is made of gold or silver, your fortune will be good. If you drink something bitter, you are being warned about a possible illness.

DRINKING GLASS: Seeing a full glass announces a pregnancy. A broken glass refers to the illness of a woman close to you. If somebody offers you a clean glass, you will have a pleasant surprise.

DROWNING: There may a tense situation in your love relationship, or you may be finding it difficult to adapt to a financial or social situation.

DRUM: If you hear a drum, this is the primal call of instinct. If you play the drum, you may be trying to gain the attention of a person of the opposite sex.

E

EAGLE: If you see an eagle flying, or if you see it standing on top of a mountain, the dream announces good times in which you will be protected by powerful people.

EARS: A warning to be careful in your communications and your actions. Cleaning your ears means to take measures to improve your relationships. Covering your ears means a lack of understanding in relationships; there is neither sexual chemistry nor positive communications at this time.

EARTHQUAKE: There are going to be important changes related to deep psychological issues.

ECHO: May indicate problems expressing your true personality when trying to communicate.

ECLIPSE: In ancient times, this dream was believed to be a bad omen. Today it is considered to be the sign of the end of one cycle and the beginning of another.

EGGS: Since antiquity, eggs have been a symbol of creativity and fertility. Broken eggs suggest fear of sterility, loss of pregnancy, sexual frustration, undesired paternity or motherhood, or fights in the family or with your partner. If the egg hatches, a new stage in life is beginning. If you eat eggs and you are not married, a wedding is on its way.

ELEPHANT: In the Hindu culture, the elephant—especially the white elephant— represents Shiva, the third person of the divine trinity and the fertility force of the Universe. If the elephant's attitude is friendly you can expect benefits, protection or help from important people. The contrary is true if the animal is hostile. Riding or maneuvering an elephant forecasts success in your activities. If the elephant chases or attacks you, it signals potential dangers or serious inconveniences. If it talks or gives you advice, pay attention to its message.

ELEVATOR: Fear of loss of social status due to circumstances out of one's control.

EMBRACE: This may forecast the departure of a friend, or it may be a warning that not all demonstrations of affection are sincere. Trust only the friends who have proven themselves .

EMPEROR: Represents the need for power, command, authority or paternal protection.

ENTRANCE: Observe your attitude in front of the entrance. If you stop, it means indecision. If you seek refuge inside, you are trying to get protection.

ENTRAPMENT: If an adult person is closed in or trapped, the dream means that you are trying to hide your human side. If it happens with animals or persons of the opposite sex, you are trying to prevent others from knowing your deepest desires.

ESCAPE: If you see someone escape, it means there are things you do not like and want to keep secret. If you are the one escaping, it may mean that you desire to escape from problems you cannot face.

EXCREMENT: Represents money. If you step on it or get dirty, money is on its way.

EXECUTION: If you are the victim, it shows feelings of guilt.

EXPEDITION: May refer to a trip or vacation you are considering. It may also represent a challenge facing you that requires a bit of preparation.

EYES: Excellent vision symbolizes clear understanding of problems and good sense, while poor vision means that dependence on others will cause you upsets. If you have eye problems, it denotes a lack of courage which prevents you from seeing things as they are. If you suffer an eye injury, someone will damage your reputation and interests. Staring at someone denotes the desire to use your magnetism to manipulate him or her, while feeling like you are being watched indicates a feeling of guilt over sexual pleasures.

F

FAINTING: This dream appears when you have forgotten your moral obligations.

FALL: Implies feelings of insecurity, guilt, or fear. A short fall means you are unprotected, while falling because someone pushes you means the possibility of accidents. Falling from a house or building represents escaping from your family.

FAN: Signifies flirtation and intrigue. People who wave a fan in a dream are longing for love. The person who waves the fan is the one who initiates sexual contact. If it is you, it is frivolous. If it is another person, then that person is looking for a clandestine date.

FARM: A farm symbolizes the administration of your finances. The condition of the farm relates to the condition of your finances.

FARMLAND (or FIELDS): If the land is dry and not well tended it indicates a need to analyze your deeper emotions. If the countryside is in good shape but not very productive, you may need to be more motivated to achieve your goals.

FETISH: Sexual fantasies. May also be a warning that people and situations are not what they appear.

FEVER: May indicate an actual fever, or foretell a change in your emotional life.

FILES, FILING: A warning about the need to use perseverance and patience.

FINGERNAILS: Represent vitality, energy, and the ability to fight. Strong, healthy nails indicate good health, a balanced life, courage and bravery. Dirty or broken nails symbolize misery, lack of courage, and illness.

FIR TREE: Represents a sincere, loyal friend.

FIRE: The characteristics of the fire determine the meaning of the dream. A fire that devours all symbolizes exalted passion, while a small, carefully lit fire without smoke represents desire, tenderness, and the need for human warmth. If you feel threatened by the flames, it suggests a fear of being overcome by an enterprise that may hide some disloyalty or flaw. If the fire burns your body, it may refer to an unfulfilled erotic desire.

FISH: If you see fish swimming or hiding among the rocks, they indicate a desire to evade responsibilities that are overwhelming you. If they escape from your hands as you try to catch them, they reflect your emotional frustrations.

FLAG: The flag represents your convictions and ideals. If you wave a flag in front of people, wealth, honor, and success are within your reach. If you are an introvert, it may symbolize the need to express your ideals without fear.

FLASHLIGHT: If you offer light to others, their advice and support may be useful. If someone offers you a flashlight, or provides light, other people may help you understand an unclear situation.

FLOATING: You may be going through a difficult situation in which you need to remain firm.

FLOWERS: In general, flowers in dreams relate to one's emotions. Each flower has its own symbolism, and the color adds another element for interpretation. Yellow or orange flowers reflect solar symbolism and express creative life and energy. Red flowers: passion. Pink flowers: romanticism and falling in love. Blue flowers: healing, intuition, and daydreaming. Purple flowers: sensitivity and maternal feelings.

FOG: You sense a problem around you but you do not know how to define it. It is a good idea to wait and see the issue clearly before making any decisions.

FOOD: When you eat with satisfaction, it means that your erotic relationship is satisfying. When the food is pleasant to eat, you will find success in your projects, but if the food is distasteful, there will be suffering, anguish, solitude, or sexual dissatisfaction. If the flavor is too strong, you may experience abuse or violence. Hot food means you need more sex to prefect your erotic techniques, and may reflect nervousness. Cold foods may show illness or health problems. If the dreaming of cold foods is recurrent, you should rethink your relationship. Cooking food means agreement in the relationship and good prospects for success. Offering food is a symbol of happiness in one's relationship, while refusing food means conflicts and struggles.

FOREIGNERS: Predicts change, and shows a propensity for unstable thinking and the need to control your mind.

FOREST: This represents your unconscious and your hidden passions or worries. Your actions while in the forest, and any people or animals you may encounter, provide clues as to the source of these feelings.

FORGET: Symbolizes a fear of death, nothingness, or emptiness; may also refer to deep secrets your unconscious doesn't want to acknowledge.

FORTUNE TELLER: Pay attention if you see a fortune teller in your dreams. You may receive special instructions to resolve issues now or in the near future. If you consult a horoscope in the dream, or cards, or any other means of divination, that is an omen of frustrations, pain, delays, or indecision. If you are the fortune teller, your advice will be very useful soon.

FOX: If the fox is chasing you, you will receive some benefits or have some type of success. Trust your judgment more than the judgment of others.

FRIENDSHIP: A symbol with diverse meanings depending on the context of the dream. If you encounter or visit a friend, it represents pleasant moments and happiness, while leaving a friend portends bad luck or failure. Laughing with a friend: separation and loss of friendship. Fighting with a friend: infidelity or misunderstandings. Helping a friend: you will receive the help you need. Seeing a friend dead: unexpected news. Seeing a friend naked: you will suffer abuse and humiliation. Hugging a friend: cheating or treason. If the friend misses an appointment: you will take part in a bad business. Seeing many friends: conspiracy, failure and harm directed toward you. If the friend is sad: sad or upsetting news and illness. If the friend is happy: happiness or good news.

FROG: If you hear frogs, they forecast gossiping and rumors, or they refer to company that we find unpleasant and hard to avoid.

FRUIT: Eating fresh fruit announces new friendships and interesting relationships.

FURY: This indicates you are going through a stressful period, and you will have to be careful not to fall into depression brought on by trying to do more than is necessary.

G

GAMES: Children's games express the desire to escape from your worries. If you cheat, it may be interpreted as difficulty adapting to social norms.

GARAGE: Represents fear of losing your possessions.

GAS STATION: May symbolize an abundance of resources, or the inner knowledge that your sexual abilities are at an optimal point.

GEESE: Represent happiness in love. If two geese are swimming or flying together it means happiness in your marriage. If you eat a goose, it means benefits and happiness at home. If the geese fly, they announce visits or news. Their screams may be a warning of danger near you.

GLASSES: If the glasses have an important role in your dream, they show the need to better observe things, people, and circumstances.

GOLD: Represents the desire for wealth rather than the actual accumulation of it. May also indicate a need to exhibit your erotic abilities in the sexual act. Finding gold represents ephemeral pleasures and imminent compulsions. To steal gold reflects family disagreements and professional conflicts. Gold jewelry shows vanity and pride, while gold tableware means fortune and power.

GOODBYE: If someone says goodbye to you, that means that you will give up a harmful habit that is creating a negative impact on your life. Maybe someone not very nice disappears from your sight. If you are the one saying goodbye that means that you will see each other again and you will be very happy.

GRANDPARENTS: Dreams about grandparents or ancestors are significant when the grandparents have already died. They are often a premonition of a disgrace, perhaps caused by you, as if it were a punishment for your spiritual or moral shortcomings. Evaluate your behavior and your moral principles.

GRAPES: You have plenty of responsibility at home and at work. A long-waited relationship becomes concrete. If you eat the grapes, you enjoy a plentiful and successful life with your partner. If you pick up grapes in a field, you will have an important position.

GREEN: Symbolizes positive actions, generosity, self-reliance, and dynamism. May also indicate jealousy, envy, and unkindness. If your health is poor, it foretells improvement.

GUNSHOT: If you hear a gunshot, your fears or weaknesses need to be examined. If you are the one who fires the shot, it means you have clear objectives.

H

HAIR: Hair is a symbol of energy controlled by will and knowledge. Seeing yourself wearing long hair is a very good thing. If the dream shows hair covering a part of the body, that represents your inner instincts. If you lose your hair, you fear aging, loss of vitality, or illness. If you pull your hair or if somebody pulls your hair, worries are nagging at you.

HAIR LOSS: Reflects one's fear of loss of virility or confusion of identity. If you see another person having body hair removed, it symbolizes that you want to get rid of some small problems that are bothering you.

HAMMER: Like other tools, it symbolizes good effort bringing positive results.

HAMMOCK: A symbol of physical pleasure, security, and comfort.

HANDWRITING (or WRITING): What you write in your dreams tells about your personality. If the writing is full of mistakes or is not straight, it shows personal chaos. Sometimes the words you read in a dream are a message sent directly from your unconscious mind.

HARASSMENT: If you are the person doing the harassing, you are about to achieve some goal you have long desired. If you are being harassed, then you may be facing a difficult situation.

HATE: If you feel hate toward someone, it indicates failure in business, rage, spite, and family disputes. It warns you to beware of intrigue and maneuvers from adversaries. It may also be a hidden fear of something erotic, such as unfulfilled or repressed sexual desires.

HERD: May symbolize the need to belong to a group and a fear of solitude. If you see a herd of animals coming toward you, you are afraid that work and responsibilities may accumulate. If you form part of the herd, you will receive great help concerning an important issue.

HEXAGRAM (six-pointed star): Union of the spiritual and the physical, or the feminine and the masculine.

HITTING: Hitting something solid is an omen of fights and conflict. The hits represent problems that you must be emotionally prepared to face.

HOLE: If you dig a hole, you may be beginning a new period in your life, or you may be trying to get to the bottom of an unclear matter. But if you fall into the hole, it means that you are creating obstacles to some type of advancement in your life.

HORSE: According to tradition, the horse symbolizes nobility and good luck. A bay horse means honor and dignity, a sorrel horse means difficulties, and a grey horse means obstacles.

HORSEFLY: There is something that bothers you deeply; may also be a premonition of danger concerning an allergy or an insect bite.

HOSPITAL: If you see yourself in a hospital, you need to make amends for infidelity or cheating. If you have not been unfaithful, you need to change partners. If you go to a hospital to see someone, it is an omen of changes in your life.

HOTEL: Uneasiness or insecurity in an unfamiliar situation.

HUMP: Having a hump is a symbol of good luck.

HUNGER: Indicates that your present relationship is not fulfilling. You may feel that your partner is not paying attention to your wishes. If you are trying to follow a strict diet, the dream relates to the hunger that you actually have in waking life.

HURRICANE: If you are calm in the face of the storm, it means you are prepared for upcoming challenges. If you are upset or fearful, it reflects your fear for problems you cannot face.

HYACINTH: Symbol of friendship and benevolence.

I

ICE: May be interpreted as coldness in personal or business relationships, or a period of waiting that seems to take too long.

ILLNESS: Worries about your health, or a need for affection and care.

IMMOBILITY: Frustration at not knowing what action to take; fear of not behaving appropriately for a particular occasion.

IMPROVISE: May reflect your fear that you have left too many loose ends unresolved in an issue that concerns you. The audacity and ingenuity you show in the dream may also come out in your real life.

INCENSE: Symbol of purity in your feelings, spirituality and finesse.

INFIDELITY: May represent discomfort with some aspect of your partner's behavior, or may suggest that you need something you are not getting in your relationship.

INFRACTION: The desire to avoid being controlled. May also be interpreted as the possibility of getting a fine.

INITIATION: Symbolizes starting a new stage in some aspect of your life; a good time to learn and improvise.

INSECTS: Associated with uncleanness or stagnation. Try to do a good cleaning, literally and metaphorically, and get rid of things you no longer need. May also represent repressed emotions; perhaps you are afraid of judgments and gossiping, or you are afraid of letting go and doing what you feel.

INSULTS: Small frictions remain unresolved in your waking life and are reflected in your dreams.

IRONING: Intent to solve difficulties in your family environment.

IVY: Symbolizes growth and attachments. Do not cling to situations since you need some distance to see objectively.

J

JAGUAR: If you are the jaguar, you have the soul of a fighter, even if you have not needed to prove it. May also be interpreted as a premonition of the arrival of a formidable enemy.

JAW: Symbolizes strength of will.

JUG: If it contains harmless liquids such as water or oil, you will have good things. If the liquids are dangerous, the omen is bad.

JUICE: Symbolizes what you are extracting from life: intuition, memory, creativity, and tenacity as well as perseverance.

JUNGLE: Symbolizes a fear of the unknown and a tendency to lose control.

JURY: Symbolizes your sense of independence and security. You may be afraid that someone will accuse you or pass judgment on you.

K

KARATE: Represents weakness and fear of attacks. Seeing it means a desire for strength and security. Practicing it means defense.

KEY: Symbolizes the double aspect of liberation and repression. A bunch of keys means acquisition of goods or knowledge. If you have trouble opening a door, it indicates difficulty achieving the objectives you have in mind.

KIOSK: If it sells publications, you will receive news soon. If the kiosk is empty, it may represent your desire to start a business or other project.

KITCHEN: Represents your emotions, attitudes, and abilities. Pay attention to whether or not the kitchen is well equipped, since that indicates your degree of readiness to confront events.

KNITTING: An omen of prosperity. If you are trying to knit without really knowing how, it means lack of creativity.

KNOTS: Represent an inability to do something. If you untie the knots, you have the capacity to resolve a problem. If the knot is messy, it shows you that you are getting into a complex situation. If you tie a knot, it may mean agreement, benefit, or good luck.

L

LABYRINTH: A symbol of hidden truth. You may be facing situations that drain your energy. If you can find the exit from the maze, it suggests that success is near.

LACE: If you see lace on a garment, you fear that someone may be abusing your trust. If you see yourself making the lace, it may show that you take advantage of other people's patience.

LAKE: If the lake is surrounded by thick vegetation, it represents feelings of love and desire. If the waters are rough, the love will be difficult and dangerous. If you fish on a lake, you are looking for a partner.

LAMP: Symbolizes external help that may be beneficial in your search for an end to your troubles. If the lamp is turned off, it may indicate that you are losing ground in a discussion or dispute.

LAVENDER: Symbolizes renovation and renewal, and may indicate a good time to do general cleaning.

LEASE (or RENT): You may be facing an unstable situation, or you may fear you are not being appreciated.

LETTER: Sometimes this may be a premonitory dream, but in general, it refers to your desire to receive news, advice, or information about an aspect of your life.

LIBRARY: Libraries in dreams signify knowledge, either acquired by studying or by experience. May represent your desire to cultivate and improve your romantic relationship and/or your sexual performance. The condition of the library, especially if it is full or empty, provides clues about your attitude toward the relationship.

LIFE PRESERVER: Your intuition is telling you that this is your last chance and you are trying to hold on to it.

LIGHT: Symbol of a spiritual path, a wealth of knowledge, and greatness of spirit. Light is the wisdom of the soul.

LIGHTHOUSE: A lighthouse with its light on indicates that you will soon find the solution or help you need. If the light is off, it means that you cannot see a way out of your problem.

LIGHTNING BUGS: Symbolize spiritual aspirations, and forecast that little by little your problems will be solved.

LION: Represents power and strength. If you are attacked by a lion, you will suffer strong opposition from someone with influence. If the lion is tame, you will help someone who is in a position of power.

LIPS: Attractive, smiling lips represent happiness, joy, family affection, friendships, and success. Pale or thin lips symbolize sadness, regrets, bad humor, and hostility. Thick lips denote confidence in yourself, honesty, deep feelings, and sincerity. Pouting lips are a sign of cowardice, indecision, laziness, and egoism. Bitten lips or cut lips may show repression and inner violence.

LIQUOR: Alcoholic drinks represent a longing for more freedom and a desire to do away with inhibitions.

LOCK: This means you are confronting a problem. If you open the lock, there will be a change of circumstances. If you close it, or if it is closed, that denotes a rejection or something that will not become a reality. If the lock breaks, the situation may be resolved in an abrupt or unexpected way. If you can peek through the keyhole, you are encountering a new situation.

LOVE: Dreaming of love means harmony and happiness at home, and satisfaction in erotic relationships. If a woman loves your husband, that means success, good luck, understanding, prosperity, and wealth. To love an unknown beautiful woman means financial gains or an inheritance on the way. To love your children implies family happiness. If you love a person of the same sex, it may suggest the need to work on your self-esteem. If it is a recurrent dream, meditate on the dream to discover your real needs.

LOVER: If someone in the dream needs your lover, the circumstances may provide clues to a situation that will affect your relationship in a negative manner. If you do not presently have a lover, there is a chance that you will soon find happiness. If you are in a relationship, dreaming of a lover may refer to fights, worries, treason, and infidelity.

LUGGAGE (or BAGGAGE): Usually it represents your emotional baggage and the unconscious desire to flee from an overwhelming situation. If the luggage is luxurious, it implies that you are satisfied with your achievements. If it is in bad condition, you feel you are a failure. If it is too heavy, you are worried about your belongings. If you lose the luggage, you fear financial problems. If you are packing a suitcase, there is something frustrating in your daily life that you do not want to face.

LYING IN BED: If you see yourself lying in bed, it may indicate a period of uncertainty or waiting in between difficulties that you cannot overcome without help. If you are lying outdoors, the difficulty is temporary and not as serious. If you are lying by a person of the same sex, or if this person is in the same room, you are worried about gossip. If you are lying by a person of the opposite sex, or if this person is in the same room, the end of your problems is approaching.

M

MAN: If a man dreams of a man with handsome looks, it is an omen of good luck, success, and achievement of your goals. If a woman dreams of a man, it means security, protection, affection, and tenderness; if the man is not someone she knows, it means a new encounter and a possible relationship. If the man is powerful and distinguished, it means success in your enterprises, support and advice. If the man is ugly or deformed, it means worries, troubles, sadness and pain, fights, illness, and failure. If he is young, it means disillusionment, upsets in business and friendships. If he is older, then it means support, protection, advice, and help. If the man is heavily-built: good luck, financial growth, productive and beneficial activities. If the man is thin: difficulties expressing yourself. To kill a man means conflicts or problems due to a lack of action or not being able to make decisions; it may also mean repression of aggressive feelings.

MAP: A good omen that you will be able to overcome your difficulties and find a solution to your problems. If someone shows you a map, a person close to you will give you good advice.

MATING: When you see animals mating, the dream may signify the announcement of a birth in the family or news about a birth.

MATURITY: May indicate a need to grow up emotionally and to analyze your fears.

MELT: If you melt gold, it symbolizes your debts. If you melt silver, it is an omen of good business. If you melt ice, it means your need to reach others through your emotions.

MEOW: If you hear a cat's meow, someone needs your attention and love. Pay more attention to your surroundings.

METAL BARS: They represent restrictions or obstacles.

MICROSCOPE: Interpreted as a need to stop and observe the small things of life.

MINSTREL: A desire for love and romanticism that you are missing in your waking life.

MIRROR: May refer to fears and desires that you cannot confess, but which require analysis. If you see yourself reflected as a deformed image, it indicates those parts of your own body that you have trouble accepting.

MISTREATMENT: May be interpreted as feeling of frustration toward life.

MONEY: Symbolizes something you desire intimately that you do not dare talk about. In dreams, it is always better to give away money rather than receiving it or finding it somewhere. If you give away money, it represents resolution of your problems. If you receive money, it almost always indicates financial or health problems.

MOON: The moon relates to emotions, femininity, and fertility. If it is full, it symbolizes abundance in love. If it is in the first quarter, it means increasing passionate love.

MOUTH: Indicates primary needs that must be fulfilled right away, as well as the capacity of expression and communication toward others. If you see yourself in dreams with your mouth covered or closed, it indicates your fear to let others know your thoughts.

MURDER: Witnessing a murder or being pursued by a murderer indicates deep fears or that you are not pleased with something in your life. If you are the murderer, you may be trying to get rid of something or someone.

N

NAIL: Finding a nail is a traditional symbol of good luck and material gains; however, the act of nailing usually indicates hardships. Hammering a nail at home may indicate an illness for a family member. If another is doing the nailing, this may suggest that someone is trying to take advantage of your trust. Being injured with a nail means difficulties with that part of the body. If you try to hammer a nail and it bends, you are not making the right decisions.

NAKEDNESS: Seeing yourself naked and feeling uncomfortable may indicate insecurity or low self-esteem. However, if you feel content, it may show that you do not have any reservations about revealing your true self. If you take off someone else's clothes, you have sexual desire for that person.

NAUSEA: You are worried, but take care not to get so wrapped up in your problems that you can't take action.

NECK (or THROAT): Symbol of stubbornness.

NEST: The need for security and tenderness in your relationship.

NUTS: If you collect nuts, it foretells that you will have a happy love life in spite of small problems.

O

OASIS: Represents peace and tranquility. If you are in the middle of some serious problems, an oasis means that those problems are ending. The distance to the oasis provides a clue to how long this will take. If you leave the oasis, you will be facing a difficult task alone.

OBELISK: Ambitious projects that will not bring the glory you dream of.

OBESITY: In spite of Western culture's obsession with thinness, obesity is considered a symbol of opulence and a forecast of earnings. If you see yourself gaining weight, you may be getting an increase in health or wealth.

OBOE: Discreet confidences or tender emotions.

OBSERVATORY: Thrilling circumstances or events, or extraordinary moments.

OBSTACLES: Fear of sexual dysfunction or impotency. If this dream is recurrent, it is possible that the dreamer is suffering from this problem. Can also be a symbol of difficulty achieving your goals.

OBSTINACY: A symbol of your determination to fulfill your objectives in waking life.

OCEAN: Symbolizes the collective unconscious with its instincts and memories, and your own emotional attitude. If the ocean is calm, so is your life. If you let yourself sink, it shows resignation. Trying to rise to the surface of the water shows a desire to fight with all your strength. Falling into the ocean forecasts a disgrace that can be blamed on you.

OGRE: Represents all you have to overcome to free yourself and expand your personality.

OIL: Oil always symbolizes success and prosperity. If you see a broken container spilling oil, the dream predicts a disgrace. If the oil leaks from a container and disappears, it means weakness and loss. If the oil has stained papers, clothing, or any other object, prosperity will be achieved by questionable means. If somebody pours oil over your head, you will be recognized above and beyond your peers. If you see oil, get splashed with it or immersed in it, good health and benefits are in your future.

OLIVE: Olives and olive oil symbolize peace, fertility, purification, strength, victory, and rewards. An olive tree or branch refers to peaceful circumstances or reconciliation.

OPENING: Sign of hope; there is a way out of your problems.

OPERA: Represents important events in the life of the person who dreams of it.

OPERATION: A heart operation is a clear warning to abandon a bad relationship even if the ending is painful. An operation on the stomach means you don't completely understand an event or situation.

OPIUM: Symbolizes costly pleasures with negative consequences.

OPPRESSION: The attitude of your relatives toward you is ambivalent.

OPTOMETRIST: If you ask the optometrist for advice, the dream represents your desire to find a solution to a painful issue. Someone close to you will provide help and support.

ORANGE: The color of strength, either physical or spiritual, controlled by the intelligent mind. It is a mix of the power of red and the mental capacity of yellow. In dreams, orange indicates noble feelings and creativity with good organization. It corresponds to new beginnings.

ORCHESTRA: If you conduct the orchestra, you need to put your affairs in order and pay attention to the personal characteristics of the people around you.

ORDER: Seeing everything, even in your dreams, in rigorous order denotes a fear of chaos.

OSTRICH: Symbolizes a tendency to refuse to accept unfavorable reality. You must have courage to face the events.

OWL: Traditional symbol of wisdom, but also related to death. The meaning will depend on how you feel toward the owl. If you scare the bird, it is an omen of illness. If you like the owl, it means you are continuing to learn and improve yourself.

OX: Symbol of patience and tranquility. If the ox is thin and sick, the dream may warn of difficult times in the future which will require lots of patience and persistence.

P

PACKAGE: Receiving a package represents hope that providential help will resolve your difficulties.

PACT: Reconciliation. This is a good time to put disagreements to rest.

PALM TREE: A symbol of regeneration and an omen that your wishes will be fulfilled.

PARROT: Someone may be gossiping about you. Be cautious with your friends and beware of confidences at this time.

PARTY: Depending on the character of the party, it may warn you about some repressed erotic desire or group sex fantasies. If there is a lot of laughter and gaiety, it may signify a period of intense unexpressed emotions.

PEACH: Represents benefits and achievements in all aspects of life, including fulfillment of your emotional and sexual desires. If you see children eating peaches, the dream announces a successful future.

PERFORMANCE: A performance at a circus, theater, or cinema says that you will acquire the things or achieve the happiness you have been wishing for.

PHOTOGRAPHY: Looking at the photos, it is possible to learn about yourself and the people and situations that surround you. Old photos relate to a desire to recapture old times.

PIG: This animal almost always refers to oneself, particularly your psychological shadow—the part of the psyche that relates to brute sexual passion or deformed basic instincts. Dreaming of pigs means you must confront your impure desires, shameful behavior, and thoughts. However, if the pig is female, especially if pregnant or caring for piglets, it is an omen of fertility and good fortune.

PLANETS: If you see any planets, it may mean that you are pondering your destiny or planning upcoming projects. If the planets are shining, it is a good omen. If they are covered by clouds or their light is weak, you may have some difficulty reaching your goals.

PLANTS: Symbolize your emotional life. If you take care of the plants, you wish to express your affection.

POLICE: Related to destiny, karma, and negative actions. If you are detained or you go to jail, it means you may expect some suffering if you cannot repay your karmic debts with positive actions.

PORT: Fear of the unknown or fear of starting a new period; may also mean a wish to disappear or escape.

POT: If the pot is full and on the fire, this foretells interesting news. If the pot is empty or not being used, it symbolizes insecurity.

PREGNANCY: Events are taking place that will result in problems in the near future, although the resolution may be very beneficial for you. Apply patience and keep your perspective.

PRIEST (or PASTOR): If you see priests or pastors, regardless of their religious affiliation, you may need to confide your problems to someone who can help you resolve them. Try to remember the advice of the character in your dream; they almost always lead you to the solution.

PRISON: Symbolizes a waiting period before changes that are coming. If you are distressed, you are not ready to confront the events. If there is a sullen guard, you may need to reflect upon events from your past that are affecting the present.

PROPOSITION: This signals the need for serious changes in your life or your morals, and can mean that you will soon meet someone or something that will change your life. If someone propositions you, your inner self needs a deep change but you are not capable of making it. If you are the person doing the propositioning, pay attention to how the encounter ends. If you are successful, it means that the moment has come for you to make those changes and sweep away anything that tries to prevent it.

PUPPY: Often related to children. Buying a puppy symbolizes getting pregnant. If a puppy gets lost, it means you are worried about a child, or it represents your dedication to your own children.

PUTREFACTION: A transitory stage that may relate to the destruction of the mental obstacles to your personal development.

R

RAIN: Emotion, fertility, purification, wealth, and abundance. If you dream of being rained on, it suggests some interference before the benefits arrive.

RAINBOW: A spiritual bridge making it possible for you to ascend to a higher state of consciousness. It is usually interpreted as hope in the face of calamities and good prospects for the future.

RATS (or MICE): They represent all that worries you, including the voice of your conscience.

RED: It symbolizes the capacity for being passionate about any aspect of life, and refers to a good spirit of combat, discipline, and organizational skill. It also represents excessive force, sometimes expressed as irritability and anger. In dreams, red appears to competitive persons, or those who have great will and a notable desire to succeed. On the other hand, it relates to all type of upsets from arrogant behavior to authoritarian conduct, or in extreme cases, self-destruction.

REFRIGERATOR: Symbolizes the larger economy, considered good or bad depending on the contents of the refrigerator.

RELIGIOUS CEREMONY: Praying is a symbol of guilt for something you do not want to accept. It may also signal that you do not know how to get out of a compromising situation and that you are expecting a miracle to resolve the problem.

REPRIMAND: If you are reprimanded, you fear that others will discover your mistakes. If you are the one reprimanding others, there is someone mocking you or your authority.

RICE: Unexpected expenses, physical exhaustion, or benefit obtained through great effort and sacrifice. It may be interpreted as future consolation that will mitigate your sorrows.

RIDER, RIDING: Symbolizes instincts, passions, and sexuality. Riding may signify a need to liberate your sexual instincts.

RIFLE: If you shoot at something, you are growing closer to reaching your goals. If you shoot up into the air, it may mean that you do not follow accepted conventions of behavior.

RING: It is said that all round shapes such as rings, bracelets, and so on suggest continuity and unity. There may also be a component of solitude or protection associated with the feeling of being inside the circle. Losing a ring indicates fights, and giving a ring to another person may reveal a desire to dominate that person, either emotionally or materially.

RIVER: A symbol of humanity and the flow of life. All goes well when the waters are quiet, but if they are rough, expect immediate complications. Murky waters indicate problems and dubious business. If the river starts on your property the dream means creativity will bring rewards. If you fall into a river, you will begin a lucky period.

ROAD (or PATH): A road is interpreted as the way your unconscious sees your destiny. A narrow road with obstacles implies difficulties and not a lot of margin for making decisions. A wide and flat road represents the freedom to go ahead with your projects.

ROBBER: This reflects fear of losing something, or of having limitations. If you are the burglar, you may be feeling remorse for taking advantage of another person.

ROCK: In general, rocks mean permanence, solidity, and endurance. If the rock looks like an obstacle, it may refer to great difficulties in your projects that you will only overcome with perseverance.

ROOM: Symbolizes your attitude toward your romantic partner and your emotional life. An attractive room represents well-being and security, while an unpleasant room symbolizes fears and frustrations. Water leaks indicate the presence of uncontrollable emotions, while cracks are an omen of future problems.

ROSARY: You are looking for supernatural protection. This dream reflects a desire for others to take care of your problems.

ROSE: A symbol of good luck, happiness, and progress. If a rose appears in the context of a love relationship, it is a sign that the relationship will prosper.

ROULETTE: The desire for a better life, but with the hope for a stroke of luck that will bring that change instead of applying your own effort.

RUBY: A symbol of emotional happiness. It forecasts an intense love that will satisfy you immensely.

RUDDER: A sense of security and a clear direction in your life.

RUG (OR CARPET): If you walk on the rug or carpet, you will be able to live comfortably on the income from your work. If the carpet is out of place, rumpled, or missing, it may indicate an unconventional job or even a risk of illegal activities.

S

SCHOLAR: If you are the scholar, you may be looking for admiration. May also symbolize your deeper Self; the scholar may help you or give you advice.

SCHOOL: May indicate tension due to a certain situation, or frustration because you do not know how to confront someone or something.

SCISSORS: Represents future fights between friends or in a marriage; or a lawsuit.

SCORE: If you see a musical score, you may be trying to understand something without success. If you are creating the score, it means the desire to plan things in a harmonious way.

SCREAM: You may soon receive good news.

SCREEN: Insecurity and feelings of shame. May represent a desire for someone that you expect to reject you completely.

SCULPTURE: If you see yourself converted into a statue, the dream symbolizes your being stuck in some aspect of the past. If you see other people converted into statues, you might be hoping for more sensitivity on their part.

SEAL: This sleek animal symbolizes sexual desire and is a sign of abundance and pleasure.

SEALING WAX: If you see a wax seal on a letter or package it represents keeping a secret or the need to seal or finalize an important situation.

SEARCH: If you are searching for a person, you are likely to hear news from him or her in your waking life. If you are searching for a particular address or location, the dream reflects your desire to change your job or place of residence.

SHIPWRECK: Symbolizes an inheritance. If the ship sinks without any violence, it means a positive change in circumstances. If the wreck is violent, a partnership or marriage may be failing.

SHOE: Putting your foot inside a shoe has a sexual meaning that relates to the desire to possess or be possessed.

SHOP WINDOW: Represents a range of alternatives from which to select. Take note of the characteristics of the objects in the window.

SHORTCUT: Taking a shortcut may be a manifestation of your desire to succeed and your disposition to set rules aside to achieve it. Pay attention to any difficulties the shortcut creates; it may show that you have an internal fear of some complications.

SIBLINGS: A warning that you must take care of your own needs. Listen to your inner voice.

SIDEWALK: The sidewalk is a zone of relative security, and in your dreams that security is always temporal and depends on what you do. If you step on the sidewalk, you have gained some security or will be offered a professional promotion that you should consider as soon as possible so as not to lose it. If you walk along the sidewalk, you are self-confident in your present position, oblivious to the fact that everything may collapse in a moment of neglect. If you step down from the sidewalk, you may be about to lose the position that gave you self-confidence, even though all seems fine right now. Ask yourself what you have done or not done that might create serious problems for you.

SIGNATURE: Represents a strong desire to get involved in a serious relationship. May also refer to the fulfillment of a deal.

SILK: This fabric has erotic connotations. If the silk is black, it means eroticism with a certain degree of sadistic fantasies. White silk relates to stable relationships, while bright colors indicate your desire to seduce someone.

SKATING: Warning of a delicate situation that will require all your ability and subtlety.

SKILLS: A new skill indicates the need to reinforce your faith in yourself. If you see yourself acting clumsily, you need to reexamine your abilities and limitations.

SKIS: The desire to take more risks and have adventures in your waking life. If you fall while skiing, it means the opposite; you are taking too many risks.

SKULL: If you hold the skull in your hands, it may indicate that you tend to exaggerate your troubles or your pains.

SKY: Represents your mental or psychological outlook. A clear blue sky means happiness, optimism, and tranquility. If the sky is grey, cloudy, or stormy, it represents worries and turmoil. The sky at night refers to events that are in gestation which have not yet come out into the open. Anything that falls unexpectedly from the sky means unfortunate or unexpected events.

SMELLS: Pleasant smells signal improvement in personal relationships in the near future Unpleasant smells or sickening odors reflect envy, hostility, negative discussions, and health problems.

SMOKE: The interpretation depends on the characteristics of the smoke. Dark, heavy, and suffocating smoke is an omen of money problems, arguments, and compromised relationships. A light, white, and pleasant smoke means relief, tranquility of the heart and spirit, pleasures, an end to worries, and approaching happiness. If you are in the middle of the smoke, it means that you cannot see your problems clearly and may have hidden enemies.

SMUGGLING: If you are the smuggler, you are afraid to be held accountable for something. If someone else is the smuggler, the dream may be showing that you do not agree with certain rules or regulations that concern you.

SNAIL: You know unconsciously that a particular situation in your life is tricky, and you are advancing at a slower pace than you would wish.

SNAKE: Symbolizes sexual character, especially in young people; can also symbolize wisdom and curative powers. Seeing a sleeping snake means that your intuition is also asleep. If the snake wakes up, you are approaching an evolutionary change. If the snake is poisonous, you may fear getting into embarrassing situations.

SOAP: Represents the need to clean and clarify. It suggest that you will see things with more clarity and the cloudy issues that you are concerned about will become plain. If you slip because of the soap, it means fear of making mistakes.

SONG: Listening to a song is interpreted as a desire to improve your reality. If the song is pleasant and harmonious, it symbolizes peace and tranquillity. If it is out of tune, there may be some conflict in the near future.

SPIDER: The spider means that your luck will soon change. If you are in a good period, things may soon start to become more difficult. If things are going badly, the spider announces new and more interesting opportunities. If you kill the spider in the dream, you will obstruct the change. If you are having a fever, when you dream of spiders the fever will come down or you will be cured.

SPLASH: This may be a warning about the possibility of being unjustly involved in a scandal.

SPOT (or STAIN): Usually interpreted as guilt. The type of spot or stain provides clues to its meaning.

SPOT REMOVER: This implies that you are going take the blame for someone else's mistake and you feel overwhelmed.

SQUIRREL: The squirrel has always represented lightness and superficiality. You may be approaching a time of many activities and a flood of small complications or upsets in your every day life. If the squirrel is free, it may announce a short-lived love.

STAGE: Being able to express all your feelings without fear.

STAIRS: Symbolizes the passing from one level to another. To go up is to ascend, to do better, to elevate oneself; it suggests transcending situations, memories, or traumas that affect your waking life. Going down represents the need to better understand yourself and the true reasons for your actions. It also suggests that you are going in the wrong direction in some aspect of your life. Sometimes the message of the dream may be found at the end of the stairs, either while going up or going down. Falling from the stairs indicates a mistake proportional to the seriousness of the fall, while the inability to go up or down portrays a period of stagnation.

STANDARD-BEARER: This means a positive or negative change at work depending on the outcome of the dream. If you are victorious, it shows that you already have what you need to perform your new responsibilities successfully. If the victory is difficult, it means that you are not ready for that responsibility, and that you may be tempted to use unethical methods to achieve it. If your side loses the battle, you must consider the possibility of rejecting an offer of work that is beyond your capabilities that could result in disaster. If you are the standard-bearer on a battlefield, you need to dominate and take control in your erotic relationship.

STEEL: If the metal is shiny, it represents success due to your own efforts or qualities, but if it is cloudy, there will be some losses. If the steel is part of a knife or sword, it is a reminder to be prudent since you are surrounded by danger.

STINGING NETTLE: Considered a symbol of treason and an omen of cruelty and suffering.

STORE ROOM: Represents unconscious desires for happiness and short-lived pleasures. If the place makes you feel uncomfortable, this may be interpreted as your fear of the consequences if you let yourself follow your inclinations.

STORK: A flying stork is a traditional herald of conception or a future pregnancy. If you see the bird landing, it may be a warning of a possible burglary.

STRAW: Preoccupation with your body. If the straw is related to another person, it may signal passivity or unsteadiness.

STREET: A wide and empty street that disappears into the horizon is an encouraging dream that shows your desire to improve yourself. The unconscious is confirming that your plans are moving in the right direction. A narrow, deserted back street has the opposite meaning, and you should study the situations you are immersed in since there may be obstacles.

SUBWAY: This dream forecasts a trying period before you see the result of your projects; a pessimistic situation or concern about the future.

SUNBEAM: May be a sign of an abrupt change on the way, or transformation in some aspect of your existence.

SUNFLOWER: May be a warning that you should focus more closely on your objectives.

SURRENDER: You feel at the mercy of others in achieving your objectives, or fear being in such a situation.

SWEARING-IN: Represents mistrust you feel toward others.

SWELLING: Represents pride and misunderstanding or a tendency to exaggerate situations.

SWIMMING: If you swim easily, it means you will have great opportunities in the future. If you see yourself drowning, it indicates difficulty in achieving your goals. If you are learning to swim, you will need to learn to control your passions.

SWORD: Symbolizes your physical strength to confront daily issues. If you use a sword, you wish to scare someone to obtain a benefit. May also mean fear of commitment.

T

TABLECLOTH: A clean tablecloth indicates prosperity. A dirty cloth warns of complications in managing your interests and the need to watch your business.

TALKING: Talking in a dream is related to your need to clearly express your desires, emotions, and sexual fantasies to your partner. It may also represent messages from your higher Self. The tone of voice and characteristics of the speech provide clues to the message's meaning. A gentle, kind voice signifies support, understanding, a favorable attitude, positive growth in your business, or fulfillment of desired goals. A strong, hostile voice or a nervous voice suggests unfavorable circumstances which will bring about opposition from third parties. Speaking with difficulty, or not being able to speak, indicates a hostile emotional or social environment that will make you feel impotent against attacks. If you speak an unknown language, or if nobody listens to you, it may be interpreted as difficulty to express your feelings in your waking life.

TATTOO: You desire recognition and want to cover a defect or weakness.

TEARING: If you see torn papers or documents, it symbolizes your desire for forgiveness in a situation that makes you feel guilty. If you tear your clothes, it is a warning of danger to your reputation, or to the reputation of the person wearing the torn clothes.

TEETH: If your teeth fall out, you fear losing your virility or growing old. If a tooth falls out and onto your hand, it may suggest a birth. If the teeth are dirty, you may feel ashamed by your family, but if the teeth are healthy and clean, they show an increase of influence in your personal environment.

TEMPER: Represents the things that you are hiding in your waking life that reappear in your dreams.

TEMPEST: A time of turbulence and change. Destiny is putting you to the test.

THEATER: Symbolizes conflicting experiences; pay attention to your role.

THERMOMETER: May indicate an actual fever. It also reveals a need to control your life and the people around you.

THROWING STONES: If you throw a stone, the dream means that you are ready to take a difficult step that may harm other people.

TIED (or FASTENED): You feel connected to or bound by something or someone. If you get rid of that tie, a change of situation is imminent.

TIGHTS: Symbol of sensuality. If they are torn, they warn you about false promises or deceptions.

TOMB: Seeing a tomb may announce a death or major life change. Building a tomb or a burial site announces an association, wedding, or birth. If you tear down the tomb, it signals the end of a difficult situation.

TOOLS: If you are using them, you will need as much help as possible in a future situation. If you only look at the tools, it means you have difficulty accepting help from others.

TORTOISE: Slowness and laziness; or patience and persistence.

TOWER: Security in a psychological sense as well as a physical sense. A solid and well-constructed tower means good defenses. If the tower is in poor condition or if it falls, it means illness or critical situations.

TRAFFIC LIGHT: Something is blocking your way. If the light is red, it may represent danger. If the light is green you can expect to receive help. If the light is yellow, don't trust appearances.

TRAIN: Symbolizes ideals, philosophies, or situations you are living now. If you miss the train, opportunities will be lost. If you get off the train, you are abandoning an ideal or a way of thinking. Suggests a change of residence or employment.

TRANSLATING: You are telling only a part of the truth, or interpreting circumstances in your favor.

TREE: Symbolizes material protection; the degree depends on the species of the tree, its strength and vitality, and whether it bears fruit. It may also refer to a desire to find out more about your ancestry.

TREMBLING: You may be under too much stress during the day and may need a break. May also be a bad return from an astral voyage.

TUTOR: The intention to adopt a discipline or pursue a field of study. If you are the tutor, you will be held responsible for other people's mistakes.

U

UMBRELLA: May show the possibility of having protection, but the inconvenience of using it represents a loss of independence.

UNDERLINE: Your subconscious is telling you that there is something important you are not considering.

UNEASINESS: A warning from your higher Self that you are not accurately perceiving things around you. Pay attention to your intuition.

UNIVERSE: Serenity of the soul and spirit. A period of rest and beneficial reflection that is good for one's imagination, creativity, relationships, and projects.

UNKNOWN: Tendency to dump your problems onto others. You do not accept responsibility for your choices.

V

VACATION: You need a rest or you feel threatened by exhaustion.

VANISH: You wish to escape from your everyday life. If another person vanishes, it reflects your fear of losing that person or of being abandoned.

VIOLET: You are cultivating generosity, and looking for a spiritual world as you travel inside yourself. This color is common in the dreams of those with sexual dysfunction.

VISIT: The need to relate to others, or feelings of solitude.

VOLCANO: Represents repressed passions that can burst, causing ruin. Controlled passions are a source of spiritual energy that is symbolized by the incredible fertility of volcanic lands.

VOMIT: You have to express what is bothering you. May also signify feelings of guilt.

VULTURE: Many books consider the vulture to be a symbol of enemies. If you identify yourself with the vulture in the dream, it means that you are well prepared to confront those who are trying to ambush you. If the bird is watching you, this is a warning that the future will bring struggles and adversity, so you must be prepared to face formidable enemies.

W

WALKING STICK: Symbol of authority. If it breaks, you may have leadership problems. If another person is using it, it refers to pressures you may be confronting.

WASHING: A sign of vitality, truth and happiness, especially if performed with clear and clean water. If the water is murky, there may be some danger or deception lurking. Washing with soap may mean you have a self-image problem.

WATER: Your relationship needs more love, with more effort put into protecting it. If the water is clear and clean, you will achieve success, financial gains, a comfortable life, happiness at home, or good health. If the water is dirty or smells unpleasant, it is an omen of threats or misunderstandings. There is a risk of fights, disagreements, and cheating. Turbulent waters mean serious difficulties, lawsuits, ill intentions, violent actions, separation, or possible illness. Water that irrigates cultivated land signifies wealth, fertility, and accumulation of goods. Water that produces a flood symbolizes an emotional burden that can cause many problems if left unresolved.

WATER NYMPHS: They symbolize the feminine, emotional quality of water, and warn of loss of control over sensual pleasures.

WATERING PLACE: Sign of tranquility and relaxation. If you see animals there, you will receive good news, a small inheritance or a donation. If the watering place is empty and dry, you will suffer minor losses. If you drink from the watering hole, which is not the best place to quench your thirst because it has been made for animals, you are not taking the right path to achieve happiness.

WATERMELON: Symbolizes fertility; may also refer to ideas or projects that you plan to put into motion with people you can trust.

WAVES: Letting yourself float on the waves is to have a passive attitude to life circumstances. Walking on the waves means having the ability to confront all problems and obstacles.

WEATHER VANE: Warns against indecision, inconstancy, and doubts about actions or ideas.

WEDDING: Attending a wedding, if you are single, means that happiness and favorable changes are coming your way. If you are married, it indicates family worries or marital problems.

WEIGHT LOSS: If you see yourself losing weight that may mean you have to take better care of your health. If you see yourself becoming very thin, there is danger of an illness. The thinner you look, the more serious the illness will be.

WELCOME: Being welcomed by a man means you will receive the protection you need. If you are unwelcome, you must not trust the advice you will receive in the next few days; analyze it very carefully.

WHEEL: You are facing a period of change, but you are clinging to the security of the past.

WHIP: Symbol of dominance and unreasonable power. It may be a warning that you are committing arbitrary actions, or you may suffer a humiliation.

WINESKIN: A full wineskin signifies abundance and an empty one, poverty.

WINTER: End of a cycle or stage. If it snows, it is a good omen that may bring you more wealth. A cold, dry winter is a symbol of aging and tiredness.

WITCH, WITCHCRAFT: Represents a tendency to blame others for your own difficulties. If you cast a spell on someone, it shows your need for unconditional love. If a spell is cast on you, you will have problems.

WOLF: The wolf shows lack of trust in yourself, insecurity, and not knowing what you want. Its appearance may indicate events or facts that have generated consequences; there may be some painful moments in the future.

WORKERS: If you talk to them, you will go through a period of great effort and dedication to improve your situation. If the workers are hostile, or if they are on strike or not working, there will be mistakes, delays, and misunderstanding.

WORM: If you see them in food, worms represent hidden corruption in situations that at first appear harmless. They may also indicate an outsider interfering in a romantic relationship.

WRINKLES: Seeing yourself with more wrinkles than normal may be an indication of certain fears or that you are going through a stage of depression. True beauty is not an external quality; the dream invites us to go deeper into our own self and cultivate our inner nature. If you see that other people have more wrinkles than usual, it may indicate a pessimistic attitude toward life.

Y

YARN: An unrolled skein of yarn implies that a new task will require a lot of effort. It may also forecast unexpected complications if you can't find the end of the thread.

YELLOW: Represents intelligence, good luck, energy, and the light of the sun.

YOKE: You have strength of will that you have not yet discovered. May also mean you have problems you do not know how to solve.

YOLK: A delicate situation. Be sensitive in handling problems.

Glossary

Here is an alphabetical list of terms used in this book, as well as others that may facilitate the understanding of the general concepts that we have discussed.

Abstinence: To totally or partially prevent yourself from satisfying your appetites, which in this case refers to the sexual appetite.

Adolescence: The period of transition between infancy and adulthood. During this stage, physical changes are produced by puberty, as well as the maturing of emotions, attitudes, and conduct implicit in the adult stage. It is during this period that young people establish their individual identities, including their sexuality.

Anal sex: A form of sexual union—heterosexual or homosexual—in which the man introduces the penis into the anus of his partner.

Aphrodisiac: Any substance or object that can enhance sexual excitement. Some stimulate the senses (sight, touch, smell, and sound) and others are taken in the form of food or drinks, medicinal mixes, and "love philters."

Brain waves: The electromagnetic rhythms in the nervous tissue of the brain. They have been classified into waves or frequencies that relate to specific conditions or behaviors: alpha, from eight to twelve cycles per second; beta, frequencies above thirteen cycles per second; delta, from one to four cycles per second; and theta, from four to eight cycles per second.

Cervix: The opening of the uterus into the vaginal canal. The cervix responds to the cyclical secretion of feminine sexual hormones, producing a mucous discharge that undergoes changes during the menstrual cycle. The cervix is firm in normal circumstances, but during pregnancy it dilates and becomes much more elastic so as to permit the baby to pass through it during delivery.

Chakra: In Sanskrit, this word means "wheel" or "center" and represents a particular concentration of energy inside the body. These energy centers are vortices related to the vertebral column and the seven most important endocrine glands. They are responsible for the coordination and vitalization of the mental, emotional, and physical bodies and their correlation with the soul, the center of consciousness. There are seven main chakras and forty-two minor ones.

Climax: The culmination of sexual pleasure: the orgasm.

Clitoris: Cylindrical organ situated at the intersection of the inner vaginal lips. It is covered by a "hood" of skin, similar to the foreskin of the penis. The clitoris is made of sensitive tissues that become erect during stimulation due to increased blood flow in the local arteries and the decrease in blood drainage through the veins. Stimulation of the clitoris is important in a woman achieving an orgasm.

Cowper's glands: A pair of glands located close to the prostate that produces a substance that neutralizes possible acidity inside the urethra —which could kill the spermatozoids—and forms part of the seminal liquid.

Cunnilingus: The stimulation of the female genital zone—including the clitoris, the vagina and its lips—with the mouth, lips, and tongue. This stimulates the woman before intercourse or as a way of inducing an orgasm.

Divination: This is the capacity to predict the future or discover hidden things by means of extrasensory perception (ESP).

Divinity: Nature or God-like quality.

Druids: The intellectual and religious caste of the pagan tribes of Europe. They saw the natural world as something sacred, especially honoring certain trees, plants, animals, rivers, lakes, and springs.

Dysfunction: In sexual terms, this refers to any problem that interferes with sexual activity.

Ejaculation: Expulsion of semen through the penis as the result of an orgasm.

Emotional body: The emotional substance of an individual.

Endocrine glands: Glands, including the testicles and the ovaries, that produce hormones and secrete them in the blood stream.

Endometrium: Internal membrane of the uterus. Serves to nourish and protect the fertilized ovum. It is also instrumental in the formation of the placenta, through which the fetus is nourished until birth.

Endorphins: Hormones that play an important role in alleviating pain and generating a general sense of well-being. Comprised of bio-chemicals and sometimes much more potent than morphine, they are very important in the processes of recuperation, since they are linked to the body's defense mechanisms.

Erection: Swelling and hardening of the penis as a result of increased blood flow during sexual stimulation.

Erogenous zones: Areas of the body that are particularly receptive to pleasure. The most common erogenous zones are the lips, nipples, genitals, inner thighs, ear lobes, neck, soles of the feet, toes, armpits, wrists, ribs, underside of the knees, and the spine. The buttocks are also an erogenous zone, but need more vigorous stimulation.

Erotic: Relating to desire or sexual pleasure.

Evolution: The spiritual and/or physical process of growing into a different or better form.

Excitement: Responses that occur in the body due to physical and mental stimulation in preparation for intercourse.

Fallopian tubes: Organs that connect the ovaries with the uterus. Once a month, one of the ovaries releases an ovum that will be carried to one of the Fallopian tubes. After intercourse, the sperm that is ejaculated goes up the Fallopian tubes, where it can fertilize the ovum.

Fantasy: In sexual terms, fantasy refers to arousing situations produced by the imagination, involving real or imaginary people.

Fellatio: Stimulation of the male genitals with the mouth, lips, and tongue.

Feng shui: Means "soft winds over calm waters," two natural forces that are indispensable for life. The contemporary application deals with balancing the energies in physical locations, and is based in its ancestral Chinese roots and the incorporation of diverse philosophies from Tibet and India.

Foreskin: Pleat of retractable skin that covers the head of the penis.

Fraenum: Small band of skin on the underside of the penis that connects the glans with the shaft. It contains lots of nerve endings and is sensitive to touch.

Genitals: The reproductive organs.

Glans: The rounded, cone-shaped head of the penis.

G-spot: Short for the Grafenburg Spot, named for the scientist that first studied it. This small zone on the floor of the vagina can produce an orgasm if stimulated appropriately. Not all women have this sensitive spot, but some of those who do appear to ejaculate during a G-spot orgasm.

Hara: This is the Japanese word for "abdomen." More specifically, it refers to a point in the center of the abdomen, a couple of inches below the navel, the location of the second chakra.

Hard: A common way of referring to the penis in its erect state.

Hormone: Biochemical substance produced by an endocrine gland. The sexual hormones—androgen, estrogen, progesterone, and testosterone —play an important role in reproductive functions.

Inner lips: Two pleats of skin situated within the outer lips of the vagina. They are more delicate than the outer lips and do not have hair. Made of the same kind of tissue as men's penises, the inner lips have numerous sensitive nerve endings.

Kama Sutra: an ancient Sanskrit text on the subject of love and sexual technique.

Kiss: Contact with the lips of the mouth that creates affectionate or sexual closeness. It can be limited to a soft mouth-to-mouth or mouth-to-body rubbing, and can include use of the tongue. Sexually, it is understood as a preliminary caress and as a fundamental element of erogenous excitement. Sexual kisses are usually given to erogenous zones and are generally done with the tongue and teeth as well as the lips.

Libido: The instinctual biological drive to have sex and procreate, this powerful force determines a large part of human behavior.

Lubricant: A slippery substance used to augment the natural secretions produced by the body and/or to diminish the friction of physical contact. It is preferable to choose water-based products with formulas especially designed to be used on the genitals and condoms, diaphragms, and other latex objects.

Magnetism: One of the forms of universal energy that influences the totality of the cosmos, from the smallest particles to the celestial bodies.

Mantra: Combination of words or syllables that, when pronounced correctly, invoke energy.

Mental waves: Waves that are produced by psychic energy in the brain, as opposed to brain waves, which are nervous system impulses. Mental waves are considered to be the medium for telepathic communications.

Mons veneris: "Mound of Venus." The front arch of the pelvis in women, above the genitals.

Multiple orgasms: As opposed to men, women can have successive orgasms; direct stimulation of the clitoris elevates the probability of achieving them. Repeated orgasms are more common during masturbation or oral sex than intercourse. In theory, all healthy women are capable of having multiple orgasms; however, the sexologists Master and Johnson estimated that only one-third of women have had them. For some women, continuous stimulation of the clitoris is not comfortable.

Nipple: Small projection of sensitive tissue at the center of the breast. This is an important erogenous zone that becomes erect during sexual excitement.

Oniric: Term that refers to everything related to dreams, fantasies, and imaginative situations that are unconscious.

Oral sex: Utilizing the mouth to stimulate the genitals of the partner, referred to as cunnilingus when a woman is being stimulated, and fellatio for a man.

Orgasm: The climax of sexual excitement, characterized by profound sensations of pleasure, and rhythmic and involuntary muscular contractions. In men, the orgasm is accompanied by the ejaculation of semen.

Outer lips: Two pleats of skin that fold over the inner lips of the vaginal opening and the urethra and extend back to the anal region. Covered with hair, they are made of the same type of tissue as the scrotum of men.

Ovaries: Female reproductive organs. Two smooth glands, shaped like an almond, about one and a half inches long. They produce and store the ovum, secrete the female sex hormones estrogen and progesterone, and release an ova every twenty-eight days.

Pelvis: Portion of the human body that includes the lower torso. Houses the intestines and reproductive organs.

Penetration: In a sexual context, this refers to the introduction of the penis into the vagina during the sexual act.

Penis: Primary male reproductive organ.

Perineum: In women, the area between the vagina and the anus. In men, the area between the scrotum and the anus.

Pheromones: Chemical substances that animals produce to communicate through the olfactory sense. There is no definitive proof that humans produce pheromones, but there are reasons to believe we do. According to Dr. Alex Comfort, of the University College in London, we have all the organs and glands necessary to create and receive pheromones, but we may have evolved in such a way as to not respond to them.

Physical body: The energetic component of the physical body composed of seven main and forty-two minor chakras, and the related network that connects all the centers and threads of energy that compose the nervous system. Also known as the etheric body.

Pituitary gland: The body's main endocrine gland, situated at the base of the brain, which secretes hormones that regulate the actions of the testicles and the ovaries.

Premature ejaculation: Sexual dysfunction in which the man ejaculates with a minimum of stimulation, often before or immediately after he introduces his penis into the vagina of his partner.

Progesterone: Female sex hormone that prepares the uterus to receive and sustain the fertilized egg.

Prostate: Small gland situated above the urethra and below the bladder in men, which circumscribes the male urethra. It blocks the exit of the bladder so as to prevent the release of urine while the penis is erect and, together with the seminal vesicles, produces the principle components of semen. The contractions of its muscles, and of others that surround it, pump the semen through the urethra and out the penis during ejaculation. The prostate can produce sexually pleasant sensations with gentle stimulation.

Pubis: The lowest part of the abdomen. It forms a triangle at the apex of the thighs, and is covered with pubic hair in adults.

Pubococcygeus (PC) muscle: Although these are various muscles, we refer to them as one group because they almost always act in unison. They are located from the pelvic floor (on the pubic bone) to the coccyx (the tailbone at the end of the vertebral column).

Rectum: The lower part of the large intestine that ends at the anus.

Refractory period: Time following an orgasm in which the majority of men, and some women, are temporarily inhibited from having another sexual response.

Reproductive system: Those parts of the human body that are directly related to reproduction.

Ritual: A series of acts or repetitive movements with a specific objective. In dogmatic and spiritual fields, rituals usually have a mystical purpose, such as pleasing a divine being, bringing luck, affecting the development or outcome of events, and so on.

Samadhi: This is the state of true yoga, in which the meditator and the object of the meditation are one. Samadhi contains two levels: 1. *Savikalpa samadhi*, identification with the essence of the object. Its highest form is the realization of the primordial substratus of pure consciousness; 2. *Nirvikalpa samadhi*, identification with the Being, in which all modes of consciousness are transcended, experimenting with absolute reality, beyond time and space.

Scrotum: Wrinkled, loose bag of skin that contains the testicles. It is situated behind the penis and hangs freely from the body, which is necessary because sperm can only be produced when the testicles are below body temperature.

Self-stimulation: Sexual stimulation of one's own body. Also known as masturbation or onanism.

Semen: Fluid that men ejaculate at orgasm, consisting of sperm produced by the testicles and the seminal liquid produced by the seminal vesicles and the prostate. The seminal liquid contains chemical substances that help activate and protect sperm. Men typically ejaculate one-half to one teaspoon of sperm.

Sexual desire: This desire evolves differently in men and women. In men, it reaches its maximum point during adolescence and gradually declines for the rest of their lives. Sexual capacity for women continues to develop until thirty years of age or more.

Sexual glands: The ovaries of the woman or the testicles of the man, also called the "gonads."

Sexual hormones: Biochemicals secreted by the glands that affect sexual characteristics and behavior in men and women. The main sexual hormones are androgen and estrogen.

Sexual roles: Roles or behaviors assumed by individuals because of one's gender.

Soul: Philosophical concept that refers to the unchangeable, eternal form of the human essence. For a long time, sexual phenomena were understood as occurring only in the physical realm, without involving the soul. The distinction between "pure love" and "erotic love" is founded in this concept.

Spasm: Involuntary contraction of certain muscles. In this context an orgasm is a type of muscle spasm.

Spiritual: Concerned with or affecting the soul. The quality of all activity that urges a human being toward some kind of positive growth—physical, emotional, institutional, social.

Stimulation: In this context, it means to provide the physical or emotional means to sexually excite or arouse.

Tantra: The combination of esoteric Buddhist and Hindu religious texts and rituals. Much of the Tantra is concerned with the liberation of psychosexual energy—the power of the wrapped serpent, Kundalini, that is located in the base of the vertebral column—through a succession of focal points (chakras), until reaching the highest chakra, the top part of the cranium, and experiencing internally the union of God and Goddess.

Taoism: A Chinese philosophical system whose followers seek to obtain longevity and physical energy.

Trance: State of disassociation from consciousness, characterized by the suspension of voluntary movements and sometimes by the automatism of activity and thought. This is a state of unconsciousness during which paranormal activity can manifest.

Transmutation: To change from one form or substance to another. The expression "mental transmutation" is generally used in spiritual literature to define the change from negative to positive thoughts.

Telepathy: The power to transmit thoughts over distances; direct communication between two minds; extrasensory perception. The existence of telepathy has been a source of contention between spiritualists and scientists for many years.

Testicles: Male glands in the shape of eggs, situated behind the penis and suspended in the scrotum. During puberty, they begin to function in two ways: they produce male reproductive cells (sperm) and the hormone testosterone, which is responsible for the development of secondary sexual characteristics, such as a deeper voice and facial hair growth.

Urethra: Tube that carries urine out of the body. In women, the urethra is very short; it extends from the bladder to the urethral opening, just in front of the entrance of the vagina. Men's urethras run the full length of the penis. In addition to transporting urine, the urethra also carries semen during ejaculation.

Uterus: Also called the womb. It is a hollow structure with thick muscular walls, about the size of a pear, located in the pelvic cavity, behind the bladder and in front of the intestine. During pregnancy, the uterus increases to five times its normal size to accommodate the growing fetus.

Vagina: Short, soft canal that extends from the vulva to the cervix, where the penis is introduced during intercourse.

Vulva: The external female genital organs are known collectively as the vulva. It is composed of the outer and inner vaginal lips, the clitoris, and the vestibular glands. The vulva can vary considerably in size, shape, and color in each woman.

Yoga: Popularly, yoga is associated with relaxation and exercise. Few people know that there is an underlying spiritual concept from the Hindu tradition. The word "yoga" comes from the Sanskrit word "yug," which means "to unite with divinity."

Bibliography

Abad, Julio. *Diccionario de sueños y misterios.* Barcelona: Editorial Obelisco S.A., 2002.

Acosta-Belén, Edna, and Christine E. Bose. *Researching Women in Latin America and the Caribbean.* Boulder Westview: Electronic Edition, Perseus Books Group, 2001.

Acevedo, Zelmar. *Homosexualidad: Hacía la destrucción de los mitos.* Buenos Aires: Ediciones del Ser, 1985.

Anonymous. *Kama Sutra y ananga ranga.* New York: Random House Español, 2000.

Baudouin, Charles. *Introducción al análisis de los sueños.* Buenos Aires: Editorial Paidós, 1997.

Belloc, Bárbara. *El perfecto sexo.* Buenos Aires: Editorial Sudamericana, 1968.

Bertholet, ed. *Dreams of Spring: Erotic Art in China.* USA: Charles Tuttle Co., 1967.

Camphausen, Rufus. José Olañeta, ed. *Diccionario de la sexualidad sagrada.* Palma: 2001.

Caron, Sue. *Nacida para el sexo.* Barcelona: Producciones Editoriales, 1978.

Carotenuto, Aldo. *Eros y pathos: Matices del sufrimiento en el amor.* Chile: Editorial Cuatro Vientos, 1996.

Chopra, Deepak. *Las siete leyes espirituales del éxito.* Madrid: Editorial Edaf, 1998.

———. *Tú eres inmortal.* Madrid: Editorial Edaf, 1999.

Clarke, Martha. *Gran diccionario de los Sueños.* España: Publisher Océano Ámbar, 1994.

Delvin, David. *Amor & sexo.* Barcelona: Plaza & Janes, 1985.

De Castro, J. *Introducción a la psicología de C.G. Jung.* Chile: Ediciones Universidad Católica de Chile, 1995.

Devi, Kamala. *Método oriental del amor.* New York: Simon & Schuster, 1977.

Devivier, Michel. *Diccionario de los sueños.* Buenos Aires: Bookseller, 1993.

Douglas, Nik and Penny Slinger. *Secretos sexuales.* España: Editorial Martinez Roca, 1999.

Evola, Julius. *El yoga tántrico.* Madrid: Editorial Edaf, 1991.

Hoffman, Lola. *Orientaciones psicoterapéuticas basadas en Carl Gustav Jung.* Chile: Editorial La Puerta Abierta, 1997.

Iam, Mabel. *El sueño del amor.* St. Paul, MN: Llewellyn Español, 2004

———. *Sex and the Perfect Lover.* St. Paul, MN: Llewellyn Español, 2003.

———. *El amante perfecto.* St. Paul, MN: Llewellyn Español, 2003.

———. *El don de la diosa.* Buenos Aires: Mega Libros, 2000.

———. *La magia del sexo,* ebook. Buenos Aires: Corpo Solar, 2001.

———. *El mito del sentido en la obra de Carl Gustav Jung.* Buenos Aires: Editorial Mirach, 1999.

Jung, C.G. *Arquetipos e inconsciente colectivo.* Buenos Aires: Editorial Paidós, 1974.

———. *Energética psíquica y esencia del sueño.* Editorial Paidós, 1982.

———. *Formaciones de lo inconsciente.* Buenos Aires, Editorial Paidós.

———. *Relaciones entre el yo y el inconsciente.* Buenos Aires: Paidós, 1987.

———. *Recuerdos, sueños y pensamientos.* Buenos Aires: Ediciones Seix Barral Sudamericana. 1966.

———. *Símbolos de transformación.* Buenos Aires: Editorial Paidós, 1982.

Gopi, Krishna. *Kundalini: El yoga de la energía.* Barcelona: Editorial Kairós, 1997.

Lama, Yeshe. *Introducción al Tantra.* Berkeley, CA.: Editorial Drama, 1995.

Levy, Howard S. and Akira Ishihara. *Tao del sexo.* Lower Lake, CA: Integral Publishing, 1989.

Lightman, Alan. *Einstein's Dreams.* New York: B & N Books, 1994.

Mokichi, Okada. *Luz de Oriente.* Atami, Japan: Editorial Lux Orines, 1967.

———. *Foundations of Paradise: Teachings for all the people.* Johrei Felloship.com. 1995.

Moreno, Maria. *El fin del sexo y otras mentiras.* Buenos Aires: Editorial Sudamericana, 2002.

Mattoon, M. A. *El análisis junguiano de los sueños.* Buenos Aires: Editorial Paidós, 1999.

Muir, Charles and Corline Muir. *Tantra: El arte del amor consciente.* Buenos Aires: Ediciones Integral, 2001.

Odier, Daniel. *Tantra: La iniciación de un occidental al amor absoluto.* Spain: Neoperson Ediciones, 1997.

Osho. *Aqui y ahora.* Madrid: Editorial Edaf, S.A., 1997.

———. *De la meditación a la meditación.* Buenos Aires: Editorial Colección Libros de Osho, 1996.

———. *Psicología de lo eeotérico.* Buenos Aires: Editorial Colección Libros de Osho, 1995.

———. *Vida, amor y risa.* Buenos Aires: Editorial Colección Libros de Osho, 1996.

Rawson, Philip. *El arte del Tantra.* Barcelona: Ediciones Destino, 1991.

Reid, Daniel. *El tao de la salud, el sexo y la larga vida.* Barcelona: Editorial Urano S. A., 2003.

Rosciano, Azima. *Chakras: Sonidos y música para regenerar las energías.* Buenos Aires: Ediciones Integral, 2001.

Rowan, Edward. *Los placeres del autoerotismo.* USA: Santillana Publishing, 2001.

Saraswati, Digambarananda. *Claves del yoga.* Spain: Los libros de la liebre de Marzo, 1998.

Samkara. *La esencia del vedanta.* Barcelona: Editorial Kairós, 1997.

Sivananda, Kalyan. *Tantra: Yoga de realización.* Buenos Aires: Edición del autor, Editorial Kier, 1973.

Tengbon, Mildred. *Hablemos del amor y del sexo.* Caribe: Editorial Betania, 1994.

Usstler, J. *La psicología del cuerpo femenino.* Madrid: Editora Arias Matano, 1991.

Varenne, Jean. *El tantrismo o la sexualidad sagrada.* Barcelona: Editorial Kairós, 1985.

Van Lysebeth, André. *Tantra: El culto de lo femenino.* Barcelona: Ediciones Urano, Barcelona, 1988.

Vatsyayana. *Kama Sutra.* Julio Lezama, trans. Colección Océano Ámbar, ebook, 2003.

Von Franz, Marie-Louise. *El camino de los sueños.* Editorial Cuatro Vientos, Santiago de Chile, 1997.

——. *Conversaciones con…* Santiago de Chile: Editorial Cuatro Vientos, 1997.

Woodroffe, Sir John. *El poder serpentino*. Buenos Aires: Editorial Kier, 1972.

——. *Principios del Tantra*. Buenos Aires: Editorial Kier, 1982.

To Write to the Author

If you wish to contact the author or would like more information about this book, please write to the author in care of Llewellyn and we will forward your request. Both the author and the publisher thank you for your interest and your comments on your reading of this book and how it has helped you. Llewellyn cannot guarantee that all correspondence written to the author will be answered, but all will be forwarded. Please send your letters to:

Mabel Iam
c/o Llewellyn
2143 Wooddale Drive, Dept. 0-7387-0825-9
Woodbury, MN 55125, U.S.A.
www.mabeliam.com

Please enclose a self-addressed stamped envelope with your address or $1.00 to cover mailing costs. Outside of the United States, use the international postal reply coupon.